CompTIA® A+ 220-801 220-802 Q&A

Chimborazo Publishing, Inc.

Course Technology PTR

A part of Cengage Learning

COURSE TECHNOLOGY
CENGAGE Learning·

Australia, Brazil, Japan, Korea, Mexico, Singapore, Spain, United Kingdom, United States

COURSE TECHNOLOGY
CENGAGE Learning

CompTIA® A+ 220-801, 220-802 Q&A
Chimborazo Publishing, Inc.

**Publisher and General Manager,
Course Technology PTR:**
Stacy L. Hiquet

Associate Director of Marketing:
Sarah Panella

Manager of Editorial Services:
Heather Talbot

Senior Marketing Manager:
Mark Hughes

Acquisitions Editor:
Heather Hurley

Project/Copy Editor:
Megan Belanger

Technical Reviewer:
Serge Palladino

Interior Layout Tech:
Bill Hartman

Cover Designer:
Mike Tanamachi

For product information and technology assistance, contact us at
Cengage Learning Customer & Sales Support, 1-800-354-9706.

For permission to use material from this text or product,
submit all requests online at **cengage.com/permissions**.
Further permissions questions can be emailed to
permissionrequest@cengage.com.

CompTIA is a registered trademark of CompTIA. Microsoft and the Office logo are either registered trademarks or trademarks of Microsoft Corporation in the United States and/or other countries.
All other trademarks are the property of their respective owners.

Library of Congress Catalog Card Number: 2013930069

ISBN-13: 978-1-285-16071-9

ISBN-10: 1-285-16071-1

Course Technology, a part of Cengage Learning
20 Channel Center Street
Boston, MA 02210
USA

Cengage Learning is a leading provider of customized learning solutions with office locations around the globe, including Singapore, the United Kingdom, Australia, Mexico, Brazil, and Japan. Locate your local office at: **international.cengage.com/region**.

Cengage Learning products are represented in Canada by Nelson Education, Ltd.

For your lifelong learning solutions, visit **courseptr.com**.

Visit our corporate website at **cengage.com**.

Printed in the United States of America
2 3 4 5 6 7 15 14 13

ABOUT THE AUTHOR

Chimborazo Publishing, Inc. (www.chimbotech.com) specializes in providing ancillary materials for textbooks at the high school, college, and trade levels, in all academic disciplines. These materials consist of Instructor's Manuals, PowerPoint presentations, test banks, distance learning content, solutions manuals, and curriculum development. All Chimborazo employees have completed an MA/MS or Ph.D. in their respective fields and have extensive experience through a combination of university courses, industry experience, and teaching. Our work has a reputation for accuracy, depth, consistency, and timeliness—gained from 12 years of developing content for more than 1,000 titles.

CONTENTS

PART III: CompTIA A+ EXAM ANSWERS

Part I

CompTIA A+
Exam 220-801

Domain 1.0 PC Hardware

Domain 2.0 Networking

Domain 3.0 Laptops

Domain 4.0 Printers

Domain 5.0 Operational Procedures

1.0

PC HARDWARE

1. When configuring a motherboard, what information is needed to find the correct user guide for a motherboard?
   A. Types and number of ports included on the motherboard
   B. Type of CPU and heat sink installed on the motherboard
   C. Manufacturer and model of the motherboard
   D. Configuration of the I/O shield and type of power source
   220-801 A+ Objective 1.1 Configure and apply BIOS settings

2. What program can easily make changes to the setup values stored in CMOS RAM?
   A. BIOS setup
   B. CONFIG setup
   C. CMOS setup
   D. I/O shield setup
   220-801 A+ Objective 1.1 Configure and apply BIOS settings

3. A new standard that is slowly replacing the BIOS standard serves as an interface between firmware on the motherboard and the operating system. It improves on processes for booting, handing over the boot to the OS, and loading device drivers and applications before the OS loads. What is the name of this new standard?
   A. POST (power-on self-test) Interface
   B. Boot Priority Interface
   C. Unified Extensible Firmware Interface (UEFI)
   D. Newer Phoenix BIOS Interface
   220-801 A+ Objective 1.1 Configure and apply BIOS settings

4. After the OS is installed, the boot sequence should typically be changed to boot first from which hardware device?
   A. DVD
   B. CMOS RAM
   C. Hard drive
   D. USB
   220-801 A+ Objective 1.1 Configure and apply BIOS settings

5. A(n) _____ is two small posts or metal pins that stick up off the motherboard that is open or closed; it is open if it has no cover and closed when it has a cover on the two pins.

A. partition table

B. parallel port

C. on–board port

D. jumper

220-801 A+ Objective 1.1 Configure and apply BIOS settings

6. Which statement is correct regarding supervisor and power-on passwords?

A. These passwords are the same password that can be required by a Windows OS at startup.

B. If both passwords are forgotten, a default password can be entered to access the system.

C. Jumpers can be set to clear both passwords.

D. Using both passwords is an alternative to flashing the BIOS when alleviating motherboard problems.

220-801 A+ Objective 1.1 Configure and apply BIOS settings

7. What term refers to the process of upgrading or refreshing the programming stored on the firmware chip?

A. booting

B. ISO imaging

C. flashing BIOS

D. firmware refreshing

220-801 A+ Objective 1.1 Configure and apply BIOS settings

8. Which statement concerning BIOS updates is correct?

A. If the update is interrupted while it is in progress, turn off the computer and then turn it back on to resume the update.

B. Update your BIOS only if you're having a problem with your motherboard or there's a new BIOS feature you want to use.

C. A BIOS update can be performed using either an earlier version or a later version than the one installed.

D. It is advisable to routinely check for updates to BIOS code posted on the motherboard manufacturer's web site and to perform updates frequently.

220-801 A+ Objective 1.1 Configure and apply BIOS settings

9. How does one access the BIOS setup program?

A. By pressing a key or combination of keys during the boot process

B. By pressing CTRL+ALT+DEL during system shut down

C. By accessing it through Control Panel after the computer is booted

D. By accessing system options through the startup login dialog box

220-801 A+ Objective 1.1 Configure and apply BIOS settings

10. What name is used to describe ports that come directly off the motherboard?
    A. External connectors
    B. Expansion ports
    C. Direct ports
    D. On-board ports
    220-801 A+ Objective 1.2 Differentiate between motherboard components, their purposes, and properties

11. What are the three most popular motherboard form factors?
    A. BTX, MicroBTX, and PicoBTX
    B. ATX, microATX, and Mini-ITX
    C. NLX, FlexATX, and BTX
    D. POST, LGA, and PCI
    220-801 A+ Objective 1.2 Differentiate between motherboard components, their purposes, and properties

12. Which of the following form factors lowers the total cost of a system by reducing the number of expansion slots on the motherboard, reducing the power supplied to the board, and allowing for a smaller case size?
    A. NLX
    B. MicroATX
    C. FlexATX
    D. BTX
    220-801 A+ Objective 1.8 Install an appropriate power supply based on a given scenario

13. Which computer component houses the power supply, motherboard, expansion cards, and drives?
    A. System box
    B. Housing unit
    C. Transformer box
    D. Computer case
    220-801 A+ Objective 1.2 Differentiate between motherboard components, their purposes, and properties

14. Which Intel socket is used in high-end gaming and server computers?
    A. LGA2011
    B. FCLGA1155
    C. Socket J1
    D. LGA775
    220-801 A+ Objective 1.6 Differentiate among various CPU types and features and select the appropriate cooling method

15. Which of the following is currently the most popular Intel socket?

    A. LGA771 socket

    B. PGA 66 socket

    C. LGA1155 socket

    D. Socket 478

    220-801 A+ Objective 1.6 Differentiate among various CPU types and features and select the appropriate cooling method

16. USB 2.0 is an example of a type of bus that does not run in sync with the system clock. What type of bus is this?

    A. Local bus

    B. Expansion bus

    C. PCI Express

    D. AGP bus

    220-801 A+ Objective 1.2 Differentiate between motherboard components, their purposes, and properties

17. Which type of bus is primarily used today and is characterized as running in sync with the system clock?

    A. Local bus

    B. PCI Express

    C. AGP bus

    D. Expansion bus

    220-801 A+ Objective 1.2 Differentiate between motherboard components, their purposes, and properties

18. Which statement regarding PCI buses is correct?

    A. The first PCI bus had a 32-bit data path, supplied 5 V of power to an expansion card, and operated at 33MHz.

    B. A universal PCI card is limited to using a 3.3 V slot.

    C. PCI- X is not backward compatible with conventional PCI cards and slots.

    D. PCI-X requires a 64-bit card.

    220-801 A+ Objective 1.2 Differentiate between motherboard components, their purposes, and properties

19. What term is sometimes used interchangeably with throughput?

    A. Boot loader

    B. CrossFire

    C. Bandwidth

    D. Latency

    220-801 A+ Objective 1.2 Differentiate between motherboard components, their purposes, and properties

20. Which of the following is focused on the server market, and therefore, unlikely to be seen in desktop computers?

    A. PCI Express

    B. AGP

    C. AMR

    D. PCI-X

    220-801 A+ Objective 1.2 Differentiate between motherboard components, their purposes, and properties

21. Which statement is correct regarding the PCI Express (PCIe) bus?

    A. PCIe is backward compatible with PCI and PCI-X.

    B. PCI Express is expected to quickly replace conventional PCI.

    C. PCI Express uses a serial bus.

    D. PCI Express buses were developed specifically for video cards.

    220-801 A+ Objective 1.2 Differentiate between motherboard components, their purposes, and properties

22. What is used at each end of the SCSI chain to reduce the amount of electrical "noise," or interference on a SCSI cable?

    A. Cable clip

    B. Cable end cap

    C. Connector apex

    D. Terminating resistor

    220-801 A+ Objective 1.5 Install and configure storage devices and use appropriate media

23. What is a transfer method that transfers data directly from the hard drive to memory without involving the CPU?

    A. ANSI

    B. DMA

    C. SATA

    D. PIO

    220-801 A+ Objective 1.7 Compare and contrast various connection interfaces and explain their purpose

24. Which of the following may include several internal connectors, including parallel ATA (PATA) connectors (also called IDE connectors), a floppy drive connector, serial ATA (SATA) connectors, SCSI connectors, a USB connector, and/or a FireWire (IEEE 1394) connector?

    A. Connector modules

    B. Motherboard

    C. I/O shields

    D. On-board ports

    220-801 A+ Objective 1.2 Differentiate between motherboard components, their purposes, and properties

25. Which statement is correct regarding a PCI riser card?

    A. Riser cards are available for PCIe and PCI-X slots; however, they are not available for conventional PCI slots.

    B. Riser cards are typically used for server computers to accommodate added storage devices.

    C. When you install an expansion card in a riser card slot, the card is positioned higher than other cards on the motherboard.

    D. A PCI riser card installs in an expansion slot and provides another slot at a right angle.

    220-801 A+ Objective 1.4 Install and configure expansion cards

26. A drive receives power by a power cable from the power supply and communicates instructions and data through a cable attached to the motherboard. Which is the faster of the two standards that hard drives, optical drives, and tape drives use for both of these types of connections?

    A. High-Definition Multimedia Interface (HDMI) standard

    B. Serial ATA (SATA) standard

    C. Parallel ATA (PATA) standard

    D. Auxiliary standard

    220-801 A+ Objective 1.8 Install an appropriate power supply based on a given scenario

27. Which statement regarding expansion cards is correct?

    A. Expansion cards add functionality to a system without generating additional heat.

    B. Expansion cards are quickly replacing less popular onboard ports.

    C. An expansion card is a circuit board that provides more ports than those provided by the motherboard.

    D. A heat sink requires an associated expansion card.

    220-801 A+ Objective 1.8 Install an appropriate power supply based on a given scenario

28. What is the term for the memory slots on the motherboard that hold memory modules?

    A. RAM slots

    B. DIMM slots

    C. HDD slots

    D. MMM slots

    220-801 A+ Objective 1.8 Install an appropriate power supply based on a given scenario

29. A hard drive, also called a hard disk drive (HDD), _____.

    A. is permanent storage used to hold data and programs

    B. requires refreshing at frequent intervals

    C. is the place where the POST program is stored

    D. typically has a heat sink installed above it

    220-801 A+ Objective 1.8 Install an appropriate power supply based on a given scenario

30. What is the main motherboard power connector used today?

A. 15-pin SATA connector

B. 4-pin Molex connector

C. 4-pin Berg connector

D. 24-pin P1 connector

220-801 A+ Objective 1.8 Install an appropriate power supply based on a given scenario

31. What type of port is capable of transmitting both digital and analog video?

A. S-Video port

B. HDMI (High-Definition Multimedia Interface) port

C. DVI (Digital Video Interface) port

D. Thunderbolt port

220-801 A+ Objective 1.11 Identify connector types and associated cables

32. What type of port is used for high-speed multimedia devices such as a digital camcorder?

A. PS/2 port

B. Ethernet port

C. USB (Universal Serial Bus) port

D. FireWire port

220-801 A+ Objective 1.11 Identify connector types and associated cables

33. What type of port transmits digital video and audio (not analog transmissions), and is slowly replacing VGA and DVI ports on personal computers?

A. DisplayPort

B. Thunderbolt port

C. FireWire port

D. Ethernet port

220-801 A+ Objective 1.11 Identify connector types and associated cables

34. When processors began to require more power, the ATX Version 2.1 specifications added a 4-pin motherboard auxiliary connector near the processor socket to provide an additional 12 V of power. A power supply that provides this 4-pin 12 volt power cord is called a(n) _____.

A. 4-pin motherboard power supply

B. 4/12 ATX power supply

C. ATX12V power supply

D. 4P12V power supply

220-801 A+ Objective 1.8 Install an appropriate power supply based on a given scenario

35. What type of connector is used for IDE (PATA) drives?

A. 20-pin P1 connector

B. 24-pin P1 connector

C. 4-pin Berg connector

D. 4-pin Molex connector

220-801 A+ Objective 1.8 Install an appropriate power supply based on a given scenario

36. What type of connector provides an extra +12 V for high-end video cards using PCI Express, Version 2 standard?

    A. 6-pin PCIe connector

    B. 8-pin PCIe connector

    C. 4-pin Berg connector

    D. 4-pin 12 volt auxiliary power connector

    220-801 A+ Objective 1.8 Install an appropriate power supply based on a given scenario

37. Wires leading from the front of the computer case to the motherboard are called the _____.

    A. BNC connectors

    B. USB connectors

    C. front panel connectors

    D. system motherboard connectors

    220-801 A+ Objective 1.2 Differentiate between motherboard components, their purposes, and properties

38. A connector leading from the front of the computer case to the motherboard, labeled as *Reset SW,* _____.

    A. controls power to the motherboard and must be connected for the PC to power up

    B. is for the switch used to reboot the computer

    C. controls the drive activity light on the front panel that lights up when any SATA or IDE device is in use

    D. controls the power light and indicates that power is on

    220-801 A+ Objective 1.2 Differentiate between motherboard components, their purposes, and properties

39. A connector leading from the front of the computer case to the motherboard labeled as *HDD LED* _____.

    A. controls power to the motherboard, and must be connected for the PC to power up

    B. is for the switch used to reboot the computer

    C. controls the drive activity light on the front panel that lights up when any SATA or IDE device is in use

    D. controls the power light and indicates that power is on

    220-801 A+ Objective 1.2 Differentiate between motherboard components, their purposes, and properties

40. What are the two major manufacturers of processors?

    A. Microsoft and Intel

    B. Intel and AMD

    C. NVIDIA and SiS

    D. AMD and NVIDIA

    220-801 A+ Objective 1.6 Differentiate among various CPU types and features and select the appropriate cooling method

1

41. The ability of a system to do more than one thing at a time is accomplished by several means. One method involves multiple processors installed in the same processor housing. What is this called?

A. multi-thread processing

B. dual-plus processing

C. multi-core processing

D. parallel-plus processing

220-801 A+ Objective 1.6 Differentiate among various CPU types and features and select the appropriate cooling method

42. Today's processors all have some memory on the processor chip (called a die). Memory on the processor die is called _____.

A. Level 1 cache (L1 cache)

B. Level 2 cache (L2 cache)

C. Level 3 cache (L3 cache)

D. Level 4 cache (L4 cache)

220-801 A+ Objective 1.6 Differentiate among various CPU types and features and select the appropriate cooling method

43. Which statement regarding static RAM (SRAM) is correct?

A. SRAM is volatile.

B. SRAM must be refreshed at frequent intervals.

C. SRAM loses its data when power is not supplied.

D. SRAM is faster than dynamic RAM (DRAM).

220-801 A+ Objective 1.6 Differentiate among various CPU types and features and select the appropriate cooling method

44. Most processors on the market today support virtualization. How is this feature enabled?

A. Virtualization is enabled through a setting made in the Control Panel.

B. Virtualization must be enabled in BIOS setup.

C. Virtualization must be enabled at the time the processor is manufactured.

D. Virtualization is automatically enabled each time the computer is booted.

220-801 A+ Objective 1.6 Differentiate among various CPU types and features and select the appropriate cooling method

45. All Intel or AMD desktop and laptop processors on the market today are hybrid processors. Which statement regarding a hybrid processor is correct?

A. A hybrid processor means that the motherboard has two processor sockets.

B. A hybrid processor is characterized by the ability to switch between threads during processing.

C. A hybrid processor refers to multiple processors installed in the same processor housing.

D. A hybrid processor can use a 32-bit operating system or a 64-bit OS.

220-801 A+ Objective 1.6 Differentiate among various CPU types and features and select the appropriate cooling method

46. Which statement regarding Hyper-Threading and HyperTransport is correct?
    A. The concept behind this feature involves having two arithmetic logic units (ALUs) installed within a single processor.
    B. The net effect is to appear as though there are two logical processors for each physical processor or core.
    C. If this feature is enabled in a system, it cannot be disabled.
    D. This feature requires the support of DDR3 memory modules.
    220-801 A+ Objective 1.6 Differentiate among various CPU types and features and select the appropriate cooling method

47. A graphics processing unit (GPU) is a processor that manipulates graphic data to form the images on a monitor screen. An integrated GPU is _____.
    A. embedded in the CPU package
    B. implemented as a video card
    C. installed on the motherboard
    D. included in a memory module
    220-801 A+ Objective 1.6 Differentiate among various CPU types and features and select the appropriate cooling method

48. Which statement is correct?
    A. The speed at which the processor operates internally is called the clock rate.
    B. The processor frequency is slower than the Front Side Bus (FSB) speed.
    C. The actual processor frequency and the clock speed can be viewed using the BIOS setup screens.
    D. The multiplier value is predetermined at the time the processor is manufactured and cannot be changed.
    220-801 A+ Objective 1.6 Differentiate among various CPU types and features and select the appropriate cooling method

49. What are the two components of a cooler that sits on top of the CPU?
    A. A fan and a thermal unit
    B. A vent and a heat sink
    C. A thermal conductor and a fan
    D. A fan and a heat sink
    220-801 A+ Objective 1.6 Differentiate among various CPU types and features and select the appropriate cooling method

1

50. Which statement regarding the thermal compound used with the cooler is correct?

  A. The primary purpose of thermal compound is to keep the fan from causing vibrations within the system.

  B. Thermal compound transmits heat better than air and makes an airtight connection between the fan and the processor.

  C. Correct application of the thermal compound results in a quieter fan operation.

  D. Newer systems have replaced the use of thermal compound with specially designed plastic clips.

  220-801 A+ Objective 1.6 Differentiate among various CPU types and features and select the appropriate cooling method

51. What is the advantage of a fan connector with four holes?

  A. There is less vibration due to a more stable configuration with the four-hole connector.

  B. The four hole connector supports pulse width modulation (PWM) which reduces the overall noise in a system.

  C. A fan with a four-hole connector runs continuously providing consistent system cooling.

  D. The fan with a four-hole connector runs at a significantly higher speed than a fan with three-hole connector.

  220-801 A+ Objective 1.6 Differentiate among various CPU types and features and select the appropriate cooling method

52. Keeping computer components from overheating via _____ consists of a small pump that sits inside the computer case, and tubes that move liquid around components and then away from them to a place where fans can cool the liquids.

  A. liquid cooling

  B. radiator cooling

  C. fluid cooling

  D. convection cooling

  220-801 A+ Objective 1.6 Differentiate among various CPU types and features and select the appropriate cooling method

53. What determines the size of the power supply and the placement of screw holes and slots used to anchor the power supply to the case?

  A. The size and placement of the processor

  B. The I/O shield installed on the system case

  C. The form factor of a power supply

  D. The numbers and types of front panel connectors

  220-801 A+ Objective 1.8 Install an appropriate power supply based on a given scenario

54. A rail is the term used to describe each voltage line of the power supply. What is the most common rail used, especially in high-end gaming systems?

    A. +3.3V rail

    B. +5V rail

    C. +12V rail

    D. +20V rail

    220-801 A+ Objective 1.8 Install an appropriate power supply based on a given scenario

55. Which statement is correct regarding power supply considerations?

    A. Power supplies that run at peak performance last longer than those operating at less than peak performance.

    B. Power supplies provide the same capacity of power over time.

    C. A higher rated power supply requires the same amount of electricity regardless of the power drawn by the components in the system.

    D. To know what size power supply you need, add up the wattage requirements of all components, and add 30 percent.

    220-801 A+ Objective 1.8 Install an appropriate power supply based on a given scenario

56. What component draws the most power in a system?

    A. Video card

    B. Fan

    C. SATA hard drive

    D. Network card

    220-801 A+ Objective 1.8 Install an appropriate power supply based on a given scenario

57. Which statement regarding dual voltage options is correct?

    A. The setting used in the United States is 220 V.

    B. The setting used in European countries is 115 V.

    C. In addition to the selection switch, the voltage selection can be made in BIOS and will be applied when the computer is rebooted.

    D. When changing the voltage selection, it is advisable to turn off the computer and unplug the power supply.

    220-801 A+ Objective 1.8 Install an appropriate power supply based on a given scenario

58. Suppose that one physical machine is hosting multiple activities that are normally performed on multiple machines. This process is known as _____.

    A. multiprocessing

    B. virtualization

    C. mirroring

    D. propagation

    220-801 A+ Objective 1.9 Evaluate and select appropriate components for a custom configuration, to meet customer specifications or needs

59. A customized system has the following specifications: multicore processor, adequate RAM (because each *machine* ties up its assigned RAM), and adequate hard drive space for each OS. This best describes a(n) _____.

 A. graphics or CAD/CAM workstation

 B. audio and video editing workstation

 C. virtualization workstation

 D. gaming PC

 220-801 A+ Objective 1.9 Evaluate and select appropriate components for a custom configuration, to meet customer specifications or needs

60. A customized system has the following specifications: a powerful processor with at least 8 GB of RAM, a high-end video card or possibly dual video cards, high-end sound card, and liquid cooling. This best describes a(n) _____.

 A. Graphics or CAD/CAM workstation

 B. Audio and video editing workstation

 C. Virtualization workstation

 D. Gaming PC

 220-801 A+ Objective 1.9 Evaluate and select appropriate components for a custom configuration, to meet customer specifications or needs

61. A customized system includes the following features: application software, e.g., Windows Media Center, HDMI port, cable TV input, satellite TV input, Internet access, remote control, SSD hard drive and a low-speed fan to minimize background noise, and a surround sound system. This best describes a(n) _____.

 A. Graphics or CAD/CAM workstation

 B. Audio and video editing workstation

 C. Home Theater PC (HTPC)

 D. Gaming PC

 220-801 A+ Objective 1.9 Evaluate and select appropriate components for a custom configuration, to meet customer specifications or needs

62. Slingbox by Sling Media represents one popular type of _____.

 A. audio and video editing workstation

 B. home server PC

 C. virtualization workstation

 D. gaming PC

 220-801 A+ Objective 1.9 Evaluate and select appropriate components for a custom configuration, to meet customer specifications or needs

63. What type of customized system would be most useful to an engineer working with CAD software to design bridges, an architect who designs skyscrapers, a graphics designer who creates artistic pages for children's books, and/or a landscape designer who creates lawn and garden plans?

    A. Graphics or CAD/CAM workstation

    B. Virtualization workstation

    C. Thick client

    D. Thin client

    220-801 A+ Objective 1.9 Evaluate and select appropriate components for a custom configuration, to meet customer specifications or needs

64. What feature is indicative of an ultra-high-end customized CAD workstation?

    A. Intel i7 processor

    B. Quadro 6000 GPU

    C. 16 GB installed RAM

    D. XenClient software

    220-801 A+ Objective 1.9 Evaluate and select appropriate components for a custom configuration, to meet customer specifications or needs

65. Which statement is correct with reference to a mid-range to high-end audio and video editing workstation?

    A. A video card that has a Quadro graphics processor is required.

    B. 8 GB of RAM is sufficient for nearly all high-speed editing work.

    C. The case form factor should be small enough to fit on a shelf in an entertainment center.

    D. Most users will require dual or triple monitors.

    220-801 A+ Objective 1.9 Evaluate and select appropriate components for a custom configuration, to meet customer specifications or needs

66. What is one reason that Windows Home Server 2011 might be considered a better choice as the OS of a home server PC than Windows 7 OS?

    A. Windows 7 does not offer a backup utility.

    B. Windows Home Server 2011 requires less hard disk space.

    C. Windows Home Server 2011 provides additional security features.

    D. Windows 2011 is more compatible with a powerful video card.

    220-801 A+ Objective 1.9 Evaluate and select appropriate components for a custom configuration, to meet customer specifications or needs

67. What type of customized system would be most likely to feature the following hardware components: Intel Core i5 processor, 8 GB RAM, hardware RAID implemented on the motherboard, network port rated for Gigabit Ethernet (1000 MBPS), a USB printer, and onboard video?

   A. Home server PC

   B. Thick client

   C. Thin client

   D. Virtualization workstation

   220-801 A+ Objective 1.9 Evaluate and select appropriate components for a custom configuration, to meet customer specifications or needs

68. What distinguishes a zero client from either a thick client or a thin client?

   A. A zero client is a low-end desktop computer or laptop.

   B. A zero client has an operating system but little computer power.

   C. A zero client is built by the manufacturer.

   D. A zero client can operate as a stand-alone computer rather than a VM client.

   220-801 A+ Objective 1.9 Evaluate and select appropriate components for a custom configuration, to meet customer specifications or needs

69. You are configuring a thin client that is receiving a virtual desktop from a server. What application would be most likely to be supported on this client?

   A. a browser

   B. a database application

   C. a desktop publishing application

   D. audio or video editing software

   220-801 A+ Objective 1.9 Evaluate and select appropriate components for a custom configuration, to meet customer specifications or needs

70. A regular desktop computer or laptop that is sometimes used as a client by a virtualization server is called a(n) _____.

   A. zero client

   B. thin client

   C. thick client

   D. intelligent terminal

   220-801 A+ Objective 1.9 Evaluate and select appropriate components for a custom configuration, to meet customer specifications or needs

71. Intel recommends liquid cooling methods for which of the following sockets?

   A. LGA775

   B. LGA1155

   C. LGA1366

   D. LGA2011

   220-801 A+ Objective 1.9 Evaluate and select appropriate components for a custom configuration, to meet customer specifications or needs

72. What is a type of memory that loses its data rapidly, requiring the memory controller to refresh it several thousand times a second?

    A. CMOS RAM

    B. DRAM

    C. RAM

    D. L1 cache

    220-801 A+ Objective 1.3 Compare and contrast RAM types and features

73. What temporarily holds data and instructions as the CPU processes them, and is stored on memory modules that are installed in memory slots on the motherboard?

    A. CMOS RAM

    B. DIMM

    C. RAM

    D. L1 cache

    220-801 A+ Objective 1.3 Compare and contrast RAM types and features

74. What type of memory module is used by all new desktop motherboards on the market today?

    A. DIMM (dual inline memory module)

    B. SO-DIMM (small outline DIMM)

    C. RIMM

    D. SIMM (single inline memory module)

    220-801 A+ Objective 1.3 Compare and contrast RAM types and features

75. SO-DIMM memory modules are used in _____.

    A. servers

    B. thick clients

    C. laptops

    D. subnotebook computers

    220-801 A+ Objective 1.3 Compare and contrast RAM types and features

76. A certain memory module has the fastest memory currently available, supports quad, triple, or dual channels, or can be installed as a single DIMM. What type of memory module is this?

    A. 184-pin RIMM

    B. 168-pin SDRAM DIMM

    C. 240-pin DDR2 DIMM

    D. 240-pin DDR3 DIMM

    220-801 A+ Objective 1.3 Compare and contrast RAM types and features

77. What type of memory module has one notch near the center of the edge connector and supports dual channels, or can be installed as a single DIMM?

    A. 184-pin RIMM

    B. 184-pin DDR DIMM

    C. 240-pin DDR2 DIMM

    D. 240-pin DDR3 DIMM

    220-801 A+ Objective 1.3 Compare and contrast RAM types and features

78. What type of memory module has one offset notch, supports dual channels, or can be installed as a single DIMM?

A. 168-pin SDRAM DIMM

B. 184-pin DDR DIMM

C. 240-pin DDR2 DIMM

D. 240-pin DDR3 DIMM

220-801 A+ Objective 1.3 Compare and contrast RAM types and features

79. What was the first DIMM to run synchronized with the system clock?

A. 168-pin SDRAM DIMM

B. 184-pin DDR DIMM

C. 240-pin DDR2 DIMM

D. 240-pin DDR3 DIMM

220-801 A+ Objective 1.3 Compare and contrast RAM types and features

80. _____, an older type of module designed by Rambus, Inc., has 184 pins and two notches near the center of the edge connector.

A. 168-pin SDRAM DIMM

B. 184-pin DDR DIMM

C. 240-pin DDR2 DIMM

D. RIMM

220-801 A+ Objective 1.3 Compare and contrast RAM types and features

81. Which statement regarding older RAM technology is correct?

A. Older RAM technology is still used for a limited number of new motherboards.

B. SIMMs are now obsolete; however, RIMMs are still quite prevalent in new motherboards.

C. RIMMs can still be purchased as replacement modules for older motherboards.

D. RAM manufacturers no longer produce older RAM.

220-801 A+ Objective 1.3 Compare and contrast RAM types and features

82. Which type of slot contains a single lane for data, which is actually four wires?

A. PCI Express x4

B. PCI Express x1

C. PCI Express x16

D. PCI Express x8

220-801 A+ Objective 1.2 Differentiate between motherboard components, their purposes, and properties

83. Which type of memory module runs twice as fast as regular SDRAM, and processes data when the system clock beat rises and again when it falls?

A. DDR

B. DDR2

C. DDR3

D. DDR4

220-801 A+ Objective 1.3 Compare and contrast RAM types and features

84. Sandy Bridge technology introduced _____, in which the processor can access four DIMMs at the same time.

    A. single channel

    B. quad channels

    C. triple channels

    D. dual channels

    220-801 A+ Objective 1.3 Compare and contrast RAM types and features

85. For dual, triple, or quad channels to work, the _____ and the DIMM must support the technology.

    A. CPU

    B. local bus

    C. motherboard

    D. system clock

    220-801 A+ Objective 1.3 Compare and contrast RAM types and features

86. Suppose a board has four DIMM slots with four DIMMs installed and has two dual memory channels, Channel A and Channel B. Which statement is correct?

    A. One DIMM from each channel can be addressed at the same time.

    B. The pair of DIMMs in a channel must be equally matched in size, speed, and features.

    C. Since all channels work together, the DIMMs in separate channels must all come from the same manufacturer.

    D. If the two DIMM slots of a channel are not populated with matching pairs of DIMMs, the motherboard will not recognize the channel.

    220-801 A+ Objective 1.3 Compare and contrast RAM types and features

87. Which statement is correct?

    A. The LGA2011 socket can access three memory slots at the same time.

    B. To get the highest performance, memory slots are placed on either side of the processor in order to shorten the length of the memory bus.

    C. Memory slots within the same channel are coded with a different color for each slot.

    D. Color coding is used to indicate the type of memory module that can be used in each memory slot.

    220-801 A+ Objective 1.3 Compare and contrast RAM types and features

88. A measure of the total bandwidth of data moving between the module and the CPU is called _____.

    A. PC rating

    B. clock speed

    C. processor speed

    D. module–CPU rating

    220-801 A+ Objective 1.3 Compare and contrast RAM types and features

89. A network printer is identified on the network by its _____.
    A. MAC address
    B. IP address
    C. NIC
    D. Ethernet card ID
    220-801 A+ Objective 1.12 Install and configure various peripheral devices

90. A DIMM with memory chips installed on both sides of the module is called a _____.
    A. two-dimensional DIMM
    B. dual DIMM
    C. twin-sided DIMM
    D. double-sided DIMM
    220-801 A+ Objective 1.3 Compare and contrast RAM types and features

91. Which statement regarding error-checking technology (ECC, or error-correcting code) is correct?
    A. A DIMM normally has an odd number of chips on the module, but a DIMM that supports ECC has an even number of chips on the module.
    B. If there are errors in one or two bits of a byte, ECC can detect and can correct the error.
    C. ECC (error-correcting code) memory costs more than non-ECC memory, but it is more reliable.
    D. It is possible to mix of ECC and non-ECC memory on the motherboard.
    220-801 A+ Objective 1.3 Compare and contrast RAM types and features

92. Which statement regarding parity is correct?
    A. Parity checking is used in newer DIMM modules.
    B. Parity checking involves a total of eight bits (7 bits for data and 1 bit for parity).
    C. Even parity occurs when the number of zeros (including the parity bit) is even.
    D. When a byte is read back from the memory module, the memory controller checks the odd or even state.
    220-801 A+ Objective 1.3 Compare and contrast RAM types and features

93. Which statement regarding a Rambus memory module (RIMM) is correct?
    A. With RIMMs, each memory slot on the motherboard must be filled to maintain continuity throughout all slots.
    B. RIMMs are slower than current DIMMs and relatively inexpensive.
    C. A C-RIMM (Continuity RIMM) has a single memory chip.
    D. RIMMs can support quad channels.
    220-801 A+ Objective 1.3 Compare and contrast RAM types and features

94. Which statement regarding memory performance is correct?

    A. The following memory modules are listed from fastest to slowest: DDR3, DDR2, DDR, and SDRAM.

    B. If you install modules of different speeds in the same system, the system will run at the slowest speed or might become unstable.

    C. When analyzing the CL or RL rating of a memory module, the higher the better.

    D. To improve performance, use single channels whenever possible rather than more complex dual, triple or quad channeling.

    220-801 A+ Objective 1.3 Compare and contrast RAM types and features

95. How can detailed information about a system's memory configuration and amount be obtained?

    A. In Windows, detailed information of memory configuration and amount is available in the System Information window.

    B. Details can only be obtained by opening the system case and examining the motherboard and memory modules.

    C. BIOS setup reports memory configuration and amount.

    D. Windows Task Manager dialog box features detailed information of memory configuration and amount.

    220-801 A+ Objective 1.3 Compare and contrast RAM types and features

96. What is the maximum amount of RAM that can be used with a 32-bit OS?

    A. 2 GB

    B. 4 GB

    C. 16 GB

    D. 32 GB

    220-801 A+ Objective 1.3 Compare and contrast RAM types and features

97. When installing adapter cards, what is the primary reason that an empty slot should be left between cards?

    A. To prevent the card from touching other cards

    B. To minimize rocking the card when fitting it into its slot

    C. To prevent buildup of static electricity when the system is operating

    D. To allow adequate airflow

    220-801 A+ Objective 1.4 Install and configure expansion cards

98. When installing a video card, error messages about video appear when Windows starts, indicating a possible conflict with onboard video. What can be done to correct this conflict?

    A. Remove and then reinsert the card.

    B. Shut down the computer and restart in Safe Mode.

    C. Disable the onboard video in Device Manager.

    D. Use Windows Task Manager to remove the error message.

    220-801 A+ Objective 1.4 Install and configure expansion cards

99. _____ refers to sound ports embedded on a motherboard.

A. Onboard sound

B. Expansion cards

C. Sound cards

D. Audio cards

220-801 A+ Objective 1.4 Install and configure expansion cards

100. An expansion card with sound ports is called a(n) _____.

A. onboard sound

B. auxiliary card

C. sound card

D. audio card

220-801 A+ Objective 1.4 Install and configure expansion cards

101. A port receives input from a TV cable and lets you view television on your computer monitor. This port is on what type of card?

A. TV capture card

B. TV tuner card

C. TV transformer card

D. TV reception card

220-801 A+ Objective 1.4 Install and configure expansion cards

102. What type of adapter card captures video input and saves it to a file on the hard drive?

A. Video capture card

B. MI (movie input) card

C. Audiovisual capture card

D. VGA card

220-801 A+ Objective 1.4 Install and configure expansion cards

103. What is the most likely sequence of steps when installing a card that captures video input?

A. 1) Install the card; 2) install the drivers; 3) install the application software that comes bundled with the card; and 4) manage the card using the applications.

B. 1) Install the drivers, 2) install the card 3) install the application software that comes bundled with the card; and 4) manage the card using the applications.

C. 1) Install the application software that comes bundled with the card; 2) install the drivers; 3) install the card; and 4) manage the card using the applications.

D. 1) Install the application software that comes bundled with the card; 2) install the card; 3) install the drivers; and 4) manage the card using the applications.

220-801 A+ Objective 1.4 Install and configure expansion cards

104. What type of monitor was first used in television sets, takes up a lot of desk space, and is now largely obsolete?

A. LCD

B. LED

C. CRT

D. Plasma

220-801 A+ Objective 1.10 Given a scenario, evaluate types and features of display devices

105. First used in laptops, what type of monitor produces an image using a liquid crystal material made of large, easily polarized molecules?

A. LCD

B. LED

C. LCM

D. Plasma

220-801 A+ Objective 1.10 Given a scenario, evaluate types and features of display devices

106. What type of monitor provides high contrast and high-quality color, is expensive and heavy, and is generally only available in large commercial sizes?

A. LCD

B. LED

C. LCM

D. Plasma

220-801 A+ Objective 1.10 Given a scenario, evaluate types and features of display devices

107. What technology provides a better range and accuracy of color and uses less power than earlier technologies, and is generally used to provide backlighting in a flat-panel monitor?

A. LCD

B. LED

C. LCM

D. Plasma

220-801 A+ Objective 1.10 Given a scenario, evaluate types and features of display devices

108. A certain monitor is used by digital cameras, camcorders, mobile devices, and other small portable electronic devices because it can produce deeper blacks, provide better contrast, work in darker rooms, and use less power than can an LCD monitor. What type of monitor is this?

A. OLED

B. LED

C. LCM

D. Plasma

220-801 A+ Objective 1.10 Given a scenario, evaluate types and features of display devices

109. What is referred to as response time, or more specifically, the time it takes for a monitor to build one screen, measured in ms (milliseconds) or Hz (hertz)?
    A. Screen rate
    B. Build rate
    C. Refresh rate
    D. Revive rate
    220-801 A+ Objective 1.10 Given a scenario, evaluate types and features of display devices

110. What refers to the number of spots or pixels on a screen that can be addressed by software?
    A. Clarity
    B. Resolution
    C. Pixel pitch
    D. Pixel count
    220-801 A+ Objective 1.10 Given a scenario, evaluate types and features of display devices

111. What term describes the number of pixels built into the LCD monitor?
    A. inherent pixels
    B. integrated pixels
    C. built-in clarity
    D. native resolution
    220-801 A+ Objective 1.10 Given a scenario, evaluate types and features of display devices

112. Monitor brightness is measured in cd/m2 (candela per square meter), which is the same as _____ per square meter.
    A. intensity
    B. lumens
    C. incandescence
    D. filaments
    220-801 A+ Objective 1.10 Given a scenario, evaluate types and features of display devices

113. What type of slot provides the fastest speed for a video card?
    A. AGP
    B. PCIe x1
    C. PCIe x16
    D. PCI-X
    220-801 A+ Objective 1.4 Install and configure expansion cards

114. What port, sometimes called a DB-15 port, is the standard analog video port and transmits three signals of red, green, and blue (RGB)?
    A. DVI-RGB port
    B. DVI-D port
    C. DVI-I port
    D. VGA port
    220-801 A+ Objective 1.11 Identify connector types and associated cables

115. What variation of DVI supports both analog and digital signals?
    A. DVI-D
    B. DVI-I
    C. DVI-A
    D. DVI-AD
    220-801 A+ Objective 1.11 Identify connector types and associated cables

116. Which statement regarding composite video is correct?
    A. A composite video port, also called an RGB port, separates the red, green, and blue (RGB) into three separate signals.
    B. A composite video port is a 4-pin or 7-pin round port used by some televisions and video equipment.
    C. Composite video does not produce as sharp an image as VGA video or S-Video.
    D. The composite video port connector is also referred to as a Din connector.
    220-801 A+ Objective 1.11 Identify connector types and associated cables

117. The Type A 19-pin _____ connector, used on most computers and televisions, transmits both digital video and audio (not analog).
    A. HDMI
    B. DVI-D
    C. DVI-DNA
    D. HDMI mini
    220-801 A+ Objective 1.11 Identify connector types and associated cables

118. A 6-pin variation of S-Video is seen on some older video cameras and looks like a PS/2 connector used by a keyboard or mouse. What is this called?
    A. Single Link connector
    B. DVI-6 connector
    C. composite video port connector
    D. MiniDin-6 connector
    220-801 A+ Objective 1.11 Identify connector types and associated cables

119. A ThinNet (10Base2) cable system uses coaxial cable with a(n) _____ connector.
    A. BNC
    B. AUI 15-pin D-shaped
    C. RJ-45
    D. ST
    220-801 A+ Objective 1.11 Identify connector types and associated cables

1

120. A Fast Ethernet cable system uses twisted pair cable with a(n) _____
     connector.
     A. BNC
     B. AUI 15-pin D-shaped
     C. RJ-45
     D. ST
     220-801 A+ Objective 1.11 Identify connector types and associated cables

121. Which statement regarding internal drive interfaces is correct?
     A. Parallel ATA (PATA) is newer and faster than Serial ATA (SATA).
     B. The two most popular internal drive interfaces are PATA and SATA.
     C. SATA is also called the IDE (Integrated Drive Electronics) standard.
     D. New motherboards sold today use only PATA connections.
     220-801 A+ Objective 1.11 Identify connector types and associated cables

122. Which of the following correctly pairs the standard with its transfer speed?
     A. ATA-7 (IDE interface): 66.6 MB/sec
     B. SATA I: 2 Gb/sec
     C. SATA II: 4 Gb/sec
     D. SATA III: 6 Gb/sec
     220-801 A+ Objective 1.7 Compare and contrast various connection interfaces and explain
     their purpose

123. Which statement regarding solid state drives (SSDs) is correct?
     A. In an SSD drive, flash memory is stored on ROM (Read Only Memory) chips inside the
        drive housing.
     B. The lifespan of an SSD drive is based on the number of read operations to the drive.
     C. SSDs are faster, more reliable, and use less power than magnetic drives.
     D. The cost of SSDs is comparable to magnetic drives for the same storage capacity.
     220-801 A+ Objective 1.5 Install and configure storage devices and use appropriate media

124. The disks of a magnetic hard drive rotate on a spindle. What four speeds are associated with
     spindles in hard drives?
     A. 5000, 10,000, 15,000, and 20,000 RPM
     B. 5400, 7200, 10,000, and 15,000 RPM
     C. 2,000, 4,000, 8,000, and 16,000 RPM
     D. 1024, 2048, 4096, and 8192 RPM
     220-801 A+ Objective 1.5 Install and configure storage devices and use appropriate media

125. What are the three sizes of Secure Digit (SD) cards, which are used in digital cameras, tablets, cell phones, MP3 players, digital camcorders, and most laptops?

    A. Full-size SD, MiniSD, and MicroSD

    B. Full-size SD, Mid-size SD, and Small SD

    C. Extended SD, Regular SD, and Compact SD

    D. Large-size SD, Mid-size SD, and Compact SD

    220-801 A+ Objective 1.5 Install and configure storage devices and use appropriate media

126. What type of flash memory card inserts in a CF slot on a digital camera, has a compact design (about the size of a postage stamp), and currently holds up to 8 GB of data?

    A. CompactFlash (CF) cards

    B. Sony Memory Stick PRO Duo

    C. MultiMedia Card (MMC)

    D. xD-Picture Card

    220-801 A+ Objective 1.5 Install and configure storage devices and use appropriate media

127. What type of RAID uses two or more physical disks to increase the disk space available for a single volume, and writes to the physical disks evenly across all disks?

    A. RAID 0

    B. RAID 2

    C. RAID 5

    D. RAID 10

    220-801 A+ Objective 1.5 Install and configure storage devices and use appropriate media

128. What type of RAID stripes data across three or more drives and uses parity checking, so that if one drive fails, the other drives can re-create the data stored on the failed drive by using the parity information?

    A. RAID 0

    B. RAID 1

    C. RAID 5

    D. RAID 10

    220-801 A+ Objective 1.5 Install and configure storage devices and use appropriate media

129. Which statement regarding RAID 10 is correct?

    A. RAID 10 requires a minimum of ten disks.

    B. RAID 10 mirrors data across pairs of disks.

    C. RAID 10 features duplexing to prevent the failure of both drives simultaneously.

    D. Using RAID 10, data is written to the first drive, and when it is full, continues to the next drive, and then on to the next as each is filled.

    220-801 A+ Objective 1.5 Install and configure storage devices and use appropriate media

130. Which statement regarding tape drives and tape cartridges is correct?

    A. Choosing the correct drive is essential since any single drive is only capable of reading and writing to one specific type of cartridge.

    B. An external tape drive is less expensive than an internal tape drive and can be used by more than one computer.

    C. An internal tape drive can interface with a computer using a SCSI, PATA, or SATA connection.

    D. The biggest disadvantage of using tape drives is the limited storage capacity.

    220-801 A+ Objective 1.5 Install and configure storage devices and use appropriate media

131. Which statement regarding floppy disk installation is correct?

    A. If the cable is connected in the wrong direction, the floppy drive light will not be lit when the drive is in use.

    B. The end of the cable with the twist connects to the motherboard.

    C. Current floppy disk drives are available as internal drives only.

    D. When connecting the data cable, align the edge color of the ribbon cable with pin 1 on the motherboard connector.

    220-801 A+ Objective 1.5 Install and configure storage devices and use appropriate media

132. You can update the drivers for storage devices or I/O devices to solve problems with the devices or to add new features. What program is used for these updates?

    A. Administrative Tools in Windows

    B. Device Manager in Windows

    C. BIOS setup

    D. Resource Manager in Windows

    220-801 A+ Objective 1.5 Install and configure storage devices and use appropriate media

133. Which statement regarding a device's speed, port, and/or slot is correct?

    A. A hard drive designed to use a USB 2.0 port will work at a higher speed if the drive is connected to a faster USB 3.0 port.

    B. A device will operate properly only if it is matched exactly to the type of port for which it is designed.

    C. A TV tuner card in a PCI slot will not work as fast as a TV tuner card in a PCI Express slot.

    D. In nearly all cases, the fastest slot (or port) should be used even if it is rated higher than recommended for the device.

    220-801 A+ Objective 1.5 Install and configure storage devices and use appropriate media

134. Which of the following is the correct ordering of ports or wireless connections, from the fastest maximum speed to the slowest speed?

A. 1) Original USB, 2) Hi-Speed USB, 3) SuperSpeed USB

B. 1) eSATA Version 1, 2) eSATA Version 2, 3) eSATA Version

C. 1) WiFi 802.11n (RF of 2.4 or 5.0 GHz), 2) WiFi 802.11a (RF of 5.0 GHz), 3) Wi-Fi 802.11b (RF of 2.4 GHz)

D. 1) Serial, parallel, 2) FireWire 400, 3) FireWire 800

220-801 A+ Objective 1.7 Compare and contrast various connection interfaces and explain their purpose

135. Which of the following correctly matches the port with its maximum cable length, or the wireless connection with its wireless range?

A. FireWire 800: up to 100 meters

B. Hi-Speed USB (USB 2.): up to 50 meters

C. Bluetooth wireless: up to 50 meters

D. Infrared (IR) wireless: up to 20 meters

220-801 A+ Objective 1.7 Compare and contrast various connection interfaces and explain their purpose

136. Which of the following correctly matches the USB connector type with its description?

A. The A Male connector on the right is square and connects to a USB 1.x or 2.0 device such as a printer.

B. The Mini-B connector on the left is flat and wide and connects to an A-Male USB port on a computer or USB hub.

C. The Micro-A connector has five pins and a smaller height than the Mini-B connector, and is used on digital cameras, cell phones, and other small electronic devices.

D. This USB 3.0 B-Male connector is used by SuperSpeed USB 3.0 devices such as printers or scanners.

220-801 A+ Objective 1.7 Compare and contrast various connection interfaces and explain their purpose

137. A network port is also called a(n) _____ port.

A. RJ-45

B. Thunderbolt

C. HDMI

D. DVI

220-801 A+ Objective 1.7 Compare and contrast various connection interfaces and explain their purpose

1

138. Which type of signal is characterized by a continuous signal with infinite variations?
   A. digital signal
   B. pulsating signal
   C. discrete signal
   D. analog signal
   220-801 A+ Objective 1.7 Compare and contrast various connection interfaces and explain their purpose

139. A PS/2 port _____.
   A. is a round 8-pin port
   B. on a PC uses the purple port for the keyboard
   C. is used by these devices: keyboard, mouse, and microphone
   D. has been replaced by FireWire ports on newer computers
   220-801 A+ Objective 1.11 Identify connector types and associated cables

140. All PATA standards since ATA-2 support the configuration of four IDE devices in a system, which is called _____.
   A. Quad IDE
   B. Dual IDE
   C. Enhanced IDE
   D. PATA4
   220-801 A+ Objective 1.5 Install and configure storage devices and use appropriate media

141. A(n) _____ must follow the ATAPI (Advanced Technology Attachment Packet Interface) standard in order to connect to a system using an IDE connector.
   A. hard drive
   B. optical drive
   C. SSD drive
   D. flash drive
   220-801 A+ Objective 1.5 Install and configure storage devices and use appropriate media

142. What type of port is a 25-pin female port used by older printers?
   A. Parallel port
   B. USB port
   C. Modem port
   D. Serial port
   220-801 A+ Objective 1.11 Identify connector types and associated cables

143. Which statement regarding the SCSI interface is correct?
   A. The SCSI bus can support up to 5 or 10 devices, depending on the SCSI standard.
   B. SCSI devices are typically used on home PCs.
   C. The only means of implementing SCSI technology is through a SCSI host adapter card installed in an expansion slot.
   D. All the devices and the host adapter form a single daisy chain.
   220-801 A+ Objective 1.11 Identify connector types and associated cables

144. Which statement regarding SCSI standards and connectors is correct?

    A. A narrow SCSI data bus has a width of 32 bits; a wide SCSI data bus has a width of 64 bits.

    B. The most popular SCSI connectors are 50-pin, A-cable connectors for narrow SCSI and 68-pin, P-cable connectors for wide SCSI.

    C. The three major versions of SCSI are Low SCSI, Medium SCSI, and High SCSI.

    D. A SCSI bus can only support one type of connector.

    220-801 A+ Objective 1.11 Identify connector types and associated cables

145. FireWire 800 or 400, eSATA, and SuperSpeed or Hi-Speed USB are common standards for

    _____.

    A. external drives

    B. SCSI

    C. secure digital cards

    D. network connections

    220-801 A+ Objective 1.5 Install and configure storage devices and use appropriate media

146. Which statement regarding IEEE 1394 connections is correct?

    A. Other names for the IEEE 1394 standard include i.LINK and FireWire; IEEE 1394 remains the most common name used.

    B. FireWire 400 (1394a) allows for up to 63 FireWire devices to be daisy chained together.

    C. FireWire 800 (1394b) supports two types of connectors and cables: a 4-pin connector that does not provide voltage to a device and a 6-pin connector that does.

    D. FireWire devices are hot-swappable, which is the ability to plug or unplug devices without first powering down the system.

    220-801 A+ Objective 1.11 Identify connector types and associated cables

147. With reference to a mouse or keyboard installation, which statement is correct?

    A. Plug a mouse or keyboard into a USB or older PS/2 port and Windows should immediately recognize it and install drivers specific to the device.

    B. For keyboards with special features such as additional buttons for Windows shortcuts, use BIOS setup after plugging in the device to customize the setup.

    C. To uninstall a USB device such as the USB keyboard, begin by clicking Uninstall a program in Control Panel.

    D. When the device is no longer needed, the first step for all devices is to use Device Manager to uninstall or disable the device.

    220-801 A+ Objective 1.12 Install and configure various peripheral devices

148. A _____, used to scan barcodes on products at the point of sale (POS) or when taking inventory, may be installed as a wireless connection, a serial port, a USB port, or a keyboard port.

    A. barcode reader

    B. digital reader

    C. smart code reader

    D. UPC reader

    220-801 A+ Objective 1.12 Install and configure various peripheral devices

149. Which statement regarding biometric devices is correct?

    A. A biometric device is an output device that outputs biological data about a person.

    B. Fingerprint readers used to log on to Windows provide strong security and may be considered sufficient to control access to sensitive data.

    C. Fingerprint readers can be embedded on a keyboard, flash drive, or laptop case.

    D. Most fingerprint readers that are not embedded in other devices use a Thunderbolt connection.

    220-801 A+ Objective 1.12 Install and configure various peripheral devices

150. Images stored on digital cameras and camcorders _____.

    A. require battery power to retain the content

    B. are typically transferred to a laptop using Bluetooth connection

    C. cannot be transferred from the device without using a cable connection

    D. on embedded memory or flash memory cards can be transferred to a PC using a USB or FireWire port and cable

    220-801 A+ Objective 1.12 Install and configure various peripheral devices

151. A webcam _____.

    A. relies on the computer's microphone because the webcam does not come with a built-in microphone

    B. must be installed as a peripheral device using a USB port or some other port because webcams are not embedded components

    C. can be installed by using the setup CD to install the software and then plugging in the webcam to a USB port

    D. requires additional software to enhance the quality of the microphone on the computer

    220-801 A+ Objective 1.12 Install and configure various peripheral devices

152. Which statement regarding MIDI devices and standards is correct?

    A. MIDI standards are used to connect electronic music equipment or to connect this equipment to a PC for input, output, and editing.

    B. A MIDI port is an 8-pin DIN port that looks like a PS/2 keyboard port, only larger.

    C. A MIDI port is typically both an input and an output port.

    D. If a PC does not have MIDI ports, a MIDI expansion board must be added to work with MIDI equipment.

    220-801 A+ Objective 1.12 Install and configure various peripheral devices

153. Which of the following statements regarding touch screens is correct?

    A. For most installations involving clamping the touch screen over a desktop monitor, you connect the touch screen to the computer by way of a USB before you install the drivers.

    B. As an add-on device, the touch screen has its own AC adapter for power.

    C. After you install the drivers and the touch screen, BIOS setup is used to decide how much of the monitor screen is taken up by the touch screen.

    D. If the monitor resolution is changed after the touch screen has been installed, the touch screen will automatically recalibrate.

    220-801 A+ Objective 1.12 Install and configure various peripheral devices

154. Which statement regarding KVM (Keyboard, Video, and Mouse) switches is correct?

   A. While a KVM switch is more expensive than using separate devices for each computer, it serves to keep desk space clear of multiple keyboards, mice, and monitors.

   B. Switch between computers by using a hot key on the keyboard, buttons on the top of the KVM switch, or a wired remote.

   C. A KVM switch requires that you install device drivers to use it.

   D. A KVM switch allows you to use one keyboard, monitor, and mouse for multiple computers; however, the KVM switch does not support microphone or speakers.

   220-801 A+ Objective 1.12 Install and configure various peripheral devices

155. What two types of slots use a retention mechanism to help stabilize a heavy card?

   A. SIMM and DIMM slots

   B. PCIe x1 and PCEI x4 slots

   C. AGP and PCIe x16 slot

   D. DIMM and SODIMM slots

   220-801 A+ Objective 1.4 Install and configure expansion cards scenario

156. A graphics tablet, also called a(n) _____, is an input device that is used to hand draw and is likely to connect by a USB port.

   A. digitizer

   B. stylus tablet

   C. illustration tablet

   D. visual tablet

   220-801 A+ Objective 1.12 Install and configure various peripheral devices

157. Which of the following statements regarding device drivers is correct?

   A. Device drivers for onboard components come already installed in a new computer.

   B. For an unstable motherboard, you can try downloading and installing updated chipset drivers and other drivers for onboard components.

   C. Device drivers are not dependent on the OS version.

   D. Device drivers are small programs stored in CMOS RAM that tell Windows how to communicate with a specific hardware device.

   220-801 A+ Objective 1.1 Configure and apply BIOS settings

158. Which statement regarding the CMOS battery is correct?

   A. If the CMOS battery is disconnected or fails, setup information stored in CMOS RAM can be retrieved if a CONFIG backup has been performed.

   B. An indication that the CMOS battery is getting weak is that the OS loads very slowly.

   C. To avoid problems due to a weak CMOS battery, replace it routinely, every two to three years.

   D. When installing a replacement battery, make sure it is an exact match to the original, or is one that the motherboard manufacturer recommends for the board.

   220-801 A+ Objective 1.2 Differentiate between motherboard components, their purposes, and properties

1

159. The Intel i800 series of chipsets use the Accelerated Hub Architecture. Which statement regarding this architecture is correct?

A. This hub has a fast and slow end, and each end is a separate chip on the motherboard.

B. The fast end of the hub, called the South Bridge, contains the graphics and memory controller, and connects directly to the processor.

C. The slower end of the hub, called the North Bridge, contains the I/O controller hub (ICH), and all I/O (input/output) devices except video connect to this hub.

D. All PCIe slots have direct access to the North Bridge.

220-801 A+ Objective 1.2 Differentiate between motherboard components, their purposes, and properties

160. Which statement regarding a TPM (Trusted Platform Module) chip is correct?

A. Nearly all motherboards on new computers include a TPM chip.

B. TPM, used along with BitLocker Encryption in Windows7/Vista, assures that a stolen drive cannot be used in another computer.

C. Initializing the TPM chip configures the chip and automatically encrypts all the contents on the hard drive.

D. Even if the TPM chip is cleared, the encryption key stored on the chip will be retained.

220-801 A+ Objective 1.1 Configure and apply BIOS settings

161. Which statement regarding BIOS setup and monitoring is correct?

A. Case and CPU fans on modern computers can be monitored through BIOS setup screens, but their speeds must be adjusted through Windows Control Panel.

B. In addition to BIOS setup, special software (e.g., TempControl by Alfredo Comparetti) is needed to monitor temperatures and voltage.

C. Event logging may be available as a BIOS setting, can log when the case is opened, and requires a cable to connect a switch on the case to a header on the motherboard.

D. Intrusion detection, which triggers an alert message when the system has been breached, is considered to be very reliable security on a system.

220-801 A+ Objective 1.1 Configure and apply BIOS settings

162. Which statement regarding dual monitors is correct?

A. For the sharpest images on both monitors, use the highest resolution selection available for each monitor.

B. Before installing a second video card, enter BIOS setup and verify that the currently installed card is configured to initialize first.

C. Installing dual monitors requires dual processors on your system.

D. When using dual monitors, both monitors must be set to the same orientation, i.e., both landscape or both portrait.

220-801 A+ Objective 1.5 Install and configure storage devices and use appropriate media

163. A(n) _____ printer connects directly to a computer by way of a USB port, parallel port, serial port, or wireless connection (Bluetooth, infrared, or Wi-Fi).

   A. default

   B. network

   C. duplex

   D. local

   220-801 A+ Objective 1.12 Install and configure various peripheral devices

164. A(n) _____ printer has an Ethernet port to connect directly to the network, or uses Wi-Fi to connect to a wireless access point.

   A. default

   B. network

   C. duplex

   D. local

   220-801 A+ Objective 1.12 Install and configure various peripheral devices

165. Which statement regarding dial-up modems is correct?

   A. Dial-up or POTS (Plain Old Telephone Service) are not recommended as an Internet connection method because of the expense.

   B. Dial-up standards are continuously being revised, and the current dial-up modem standard is the V.2012 standard.

   C. Modem cards in desktop computers provide two phone jacks, called RJ-11 jacks.

   D. Used when connecting a simple telephone to the modem, phone cords are a type of twisted-pair cable and use an RJ-45 connector.

   220-801 A+ Objective 1.11 Identify connector types and associated cables

166. Which statement regarding file systems is correct?

   A. File systems are only required for large capacity storage devices, e.g., hard drives and high-capacity USBs.

   B. The exFAT file system is primarily used by hard drives.

   C. The NTFS file system (New Technology file system) is used by removable storage devices such as large-capacity USB flash drives and large-capacity memory cards.

   D. Installing a new file system on a device is called formatting the device, and this process erases all data on the device.

   220-801 A+ Objective 1.5 Install and configure storage devices and use appropriate media

167. _____, which can be managed in the Windows 7 Devices and Printers window, is the process of placing print jobs in a print queue so that an application can be released from the printing process before printing is completed.

   A. Spooling

   B. Queuing

   C. Stacking

   D. Backlogging

   220-801 A+ Objective 1.12 Install and configure various peripheral devices

168. After a printer is installed, use the printer's _____ dialog box to manage printer features (e.g., paper size installed in each input tray bin) and hardware devices (e.g., stapler or stacker unit) installed on the printer.

A. Preferences

B. Configuration

C. Properties

D. Setup

220-801 A+ Objective 1.12 Install and configure various peripheral devices

169. Which statement about the categories of parallel ports is correct?

A. Standard Parallel Port (SPP) transmits in only one direction, to where the printer can communicate with the computer.

B. ECP (Extended Capabilities Port) is faster than an EPP port.

C. EPP (Enhanced Parallel Port) communicates in only one direction, but is much faster than SPP.

D. A parallel port is sometimes called a Centronics port, named after the 36-pin Centronics connection used by printers.

220-801 A+ Objective 1.12 Install and configure various peripheral devices

170. Which of the following actions should be considered or pursued if a problem occurs with an installation using a parallel port?

A. Use printer Properties dialog box to ensure that the port is enabled.

B. Use Device Manager to determine if the port is configured correctly.

C. Use BIOS setup to make sure the OS recognizes the port without an error.

D. Consider that there might a problem with the parallel cable.

220-801 A+ Objective 1.12 Install and configure various peripheral devices

171. If the processor requests something from a slow device and the device is not ready, the device issues a(n) _____, which is a command to the processor to wait for slower devices to catch up.

A. frequency state

B. wait state

C. latency state

D. idle state

220-801 A+ Objective 1.2 Differentiate between motherboard components, their purposes, and properties

172. _____ is the term for a set of chips on the motherboard that works closely (and is compatible) with the processor in order to collectively control the memory, buses on the motherboard, and some peripherals.

   A. Chipset

   B. Interface chips

   C. Control chips

   D. Hub chips

   220-801 A+ Objective 1.2 Differentiate between motherboard components, their purposes, and properties

173. Which statement regarding the system clock and system operations is correct?

   A. The chipset sends out a continuous analog signal on one line of the system bus.

   B. The pulse carried by the system clock line is read by other components on the motherboard and ensures that all activities are synchronized.

   C. Each device works on a clock cycle or beat of the clock performing exactly one operation for each beat of the clock.

   D. The CPU, bus, and other devices work in a non-stop, continuous fashion to perform commands or move data.

   220-801 A+ Objective 1.2 Differentiate between motherboard components, their purposes, and properties

174. What units are used to measure the speed of memory, the Front Side Bus, or the processor?

   A. GT/s

   B. bps

   C. pps

   D. MHz or GHz

   220-801 A+ Objective 1.2 Differentiate between motherboard components, their purposes, and properties

175. What is the width of a bus (e.g., 8, 16, 32, 74, and 128 bits) called?

   A. data transfer width

   B. bit width

   C. data path size

   D. data transfer width

   220-801 A+ Objective 1.2 Differentiate between motherboard components, their purposes, and properties

2.0

NETWORKING

1. Most communication between computers on a network or the Internet uses the
   _____ model.
   A. multicast
   B. peer-to-peer
   C. client/server
   D. multicast
   220-801 A+ Objective 2.3 Explain properties and characteristics of TCP/IP

2. What term is used to describe the methods and rules used for communication?
   A. Standards
   B. Guidelines
   C. Models
   D. Protocols
   220-801 A+ Objective 2.3 Explain properties and characteristics of TCP/IP

3. When data is transmitted on a network, what information is stored in a packet?
   A. Bandwidth
   B. Payload
   C. Data throughput
   D. Protocols
   220-801 A+ Objective 2.3 Explain properties and characteristics of TCP/IP

4. Before data is transmitted on a network, it is first broken up into _____.
   A. octets
   B. segments
   C. subnets
   D. switches
   220-801 A+ Objective 2.3 Explain properties and characteristics of TCP/IP

5. What term describes any device or computer that network traffic can use to leave one net-
   work and go to a different network?
   A. NIC
   B. Switch
   C. Gateway
   D. Network card
   220-801 A+ Objective 2.3 Explain properties and characteristics of TCP/IP

6. What is a six-byte number that uniquely identifies a network adapter?
   A. IP address
   B. Access point
   C. MAC address
   D. Port address
   220-801 A+ Objective 2.3 Explain properties and characteristics of TCP/IP

7. What device manages traffic between two or more networks and can help find the best path for traffic to get from one network to another?
   A. Router
   B. Gateway
   C. Hub
   D. Port
   220-801 A+ Objective 2.3 Explain properties and characteristics of TCP/IP

8. Which of the following is a network bound by routers or other gateway devices?
   A. LAN
   B. Subnet
   C. SMTP
   D. Wi-Fi
   220-801 A+ Objective 2.3 Explain properties and characteristics of TCP/IP

9. Computers on the same LAN communicate using _____.
   A. port addresses
   B. MAC addresses
   C. IP addresses
   D. Ethernet addresses
   220-801 A+ Objective 2.3 Explain properties and characteristics of TCP/IP

10. Computers on different LANs communicate over the Internet using _____.
    A. Ethernet addresses
    B. MAC addresses
    C. IP addresses
    D. port addresses
    220-801 A+ Objective 2.3 Explain properties and characteristics of TCP/IP

11. Which of the following is a 32-bit or 128-bit string that is assigned to a network connection when a connection is first made?
    A. Access point
    B. MAC address
    C. Port address
    D. IP address
    220-801 A+ Objective 2.3 Explain properties and characteristics of TCP/IP

12. A private network that uses TCP/IP protocols is called a(n) _____.
    A. access point
    B. intranet
    C. client/server network
    D. peer-to-peer network
    220-801 A+ Objective 2.3 Explain properties and characteristics of TCP/IP

13. Suppose that several local networks are tied together in a subsystem of a larger intranet. What term refers to this group of small local networks?
    A. Subnet
    B. Port
    C. Segment
    D. DMZ
    220-801 A+ Objective 2.3 Explain properties and characteristics of TCP/IP

14. Each client and server application installed on a computer listens at a predetermined address that uniquely identifies the application on the computer. What is this address called?
    A. Access point
    B. MAC address
    C. Port address
    D. IP address
    220-801 A+ Objective 2.3 Explain properties and characteristics of TCP/IP

15. Which statement regarding IP/MAC addresses is correct?
    A. An IP address is embedded on a network adapter at the factory.
    B. MAC addresses are assigned manually or by software.
    C. A dynamic IP address is assigned by a server each time it connects to the network.
    D. A dynamic IP address is permanently assigned to the computer or device.
    220-801 A+ Objective 2.3 Explain properties and characteristics of TCP/IP

16. A computer attempts to initiate a connection to a network and request an IP address. Which of the following provides this address?
    A. Web server
    B. Web browser
    C. Email server
    D. DHCP server
    220-801 A+ Objective 2.3 Explain properties and characteristics of TCP/IP

17. 1A computer or other device (such as a network printer) that requests an address from a DHCP server is called a _____.
    A. DHCP client
    B. neighbor port
    C. subnet server
    D. DHCP host
    220-801 A+ Objective 2.3 Explain properties and characteristics of TCP/IP

18. Which statement regarding IP addresses is correct?

    A. An IP address has 36 bits or 148 bits.

    B. Internet Protocol version 4 (IPv4) uses an IP address with 128 bits.

    C. The Internet Assigned Numbers Authority is responsible for keeping track of assigned IP addresses.

    D. A 32-bit IP address is organized into two groups of 16 bits each.

    220-801 A+ Objective 2.3 Explain properties and characteristics of TCP/IP

19. Which statement regarding the portions of an IP address is correct?

    A. The largest possible 8-bit number is 1111111.

    B. The first part of an IP address identifies the host.

    C. The last part of an IP address identifies the network.

    D. When data is routed over the Internet, the network portion of the IP address is used to locate the right network.

    220-801 A+ Objective 2.3 Explain properties and characteristics of TCP/IP

20. The IP address 150.35.0.1 belongs to which class?

    A. Class A

    B. Class B

    C. Class C

    D. Class D

    220-801 A+ Objective 2.3 Explain properties and characteristics of TCP/IP

21. The IP address 200.80.15.1 belongs to which class?

    A. Class A

    B. Class B

    C. Class C

    D. Class D

    220-801 A+ Objective 2.3 Explain properties and characteristics of TCP/IP

22. What class is used for multicasting?

    A. Class A

    B. Class B

    C. Class C

    D. Class D

    220-801 A+ Objective 2.3 Explain properties and characteristics of TCP/IP

23. Which of the following is considered a loopback address?

    A. 255.255.255.255

    B. 0.0.0.0

    C. 127.0.0.1

    D. 150.35.0.3

    220-801 A+ Objective 2.3 Explain properties and characteristics of TCP/IP

24. Consider a string of ones followed by a string of zeros. The ones say, "On our network, this part of an IP address is the network part," and the group of zeros says, "On our network, this part of an IP address is the host part." What is this address called?

A. Subnet mask

B. Packet

C. Octet

D. Subnet ID

220-801 A+ Objective 2.3 Explain properties and characteristics of TCP/IP

25. Which of the following is used with IPv4 to identify the network and host portions of an IP address?

A. Subnet ID

B. Hosts file

C. Subnet mask

D. Loopback address

220-801 A+ Objective 2.3 Explain properties and characteristics of TCP/IP

26. Which two computers are in the same subnet?

A. 15.50.212.59 and 15.50.235.80

B. 15.50.212.59 and 15.50.220.100

C. 89.100.135.78 and89.100.155.78

D. 201.18.20.208 and 201.18.35.208

220-801 A+ Objective 2.3 Explain properties and characteristics of TCP/IP

27. IP addresses that are available to the Internet are called _____.

A. Subnet masks

B. MAC addresses

C. Host addresses

D. Public IP addresses

220-801 A+ Objective 2.3 Explain properties and characteristics of TCP/IP

28. What is a TCP/IP protocol that substitutes the public IP address of the router for the private IP address of the other computer when these computers need to communicate on the Internet?

A. SNMP

B. NAT

C. DHCP

D. FTP

220-801 A+ Objective 2.3 Explain properties and characteristics of TCP/IP

29. Which statement regarding Internet standards is correct?

    A. ICANN, a nonprofit organization, is responsible for many Internet standards.

    B. Internet standards are proposed to the networking community in the form of an RFC (Request for Comment).

    C. IEEE 1918 outlines recommendations for private IP addresses.

    D. The IP addresses 192.168.0.0 through 192.168.255.255 are reserved for public networks.

    220-801 A+ Objective 2.3 Explain properties and characteristics of TCP/IP

30. What term refers to a local area network (LAN) or wide area network (WAN) bounded by routers?

    A. Neighbor

    B. Interface ID

    C. Link

    D. Interface

    220-801 A+ Objective 2.3 Explain properties and characteristics of TCP/IP

31. What is a node's attachment to a link?

    A. Neighbor

    B. Interface ID

    C. Node point

    D. Interface

    220-801 A+ Objective 2.3 Explain properties and characteristics of TCP/IP

32. The last 64 bits or 4 blocks of an IP address that identifies the interface is called a(n) _____.

    A. neighbor

    B. interface ID

    C. link

    D. access ID

    220-801 A+ Objective 2.3 Explain properties and characteristics of TCP/IP

33. Which statement regarding networked computers is correct?

    A. If a computer first connects to a network and is unable to lease an IP address from the DHCP server, it uses an Automatic Private IP Address (APIPA) in the address range 169.254.x.y.

    B. A computer with an IPv4 address has 128 bits that are written as eight blocks of hexadecimal numbers separated by colons.

    C. A computer using a private IP address on a private network can still access the Internet if a router or other device that stands between the network and the Internet is using FQDN.

    D. Neighbors are two or more nodes on the same port.

    220-801 A+ Objective 2.3 Explain properties and characteristics of TCP/IP

34. What protocol was developed for IPv6 packets to travel over an IPv4 network?

A. Teredo

B. TCP/IP

C. DHCP

D. Telnet

220-801 A+ Objective 2.3 Explain properties and characteristics of TCP/IP

35. What identifies a single interface on a network?

A. Multicast address

B. Subnet ID

C. Port address

D. Unicast address

220-801 A+ Objective 2.3 Explain properties and characteristics of TCP/IP

36. Which statement regarding local and global addresses is correct?

A. A link–local address is used to identify a specific site within a large organization.

B. A global unicast address cannot be routed on the Internet.

C. Link–local addresses are allowed on the Internet.

D. A local link is a subnet.

220-801 A+ Objective 2.3 Explain properties and characteristics of TCP/IP

37. What address prefix is used for most global unicast addresses?

A. 2000::/3

B. FC00::/7

C. FE80::/64

D. FF00::/8

220-801 A+ Objective 2.3 Explain properties and characteristics of TCP/IP

38. Most multicast addresses use which of the following address prefixes?

A. 2000::/3

B. FC00::/7

C. FE80::/64

D. FF00::/8

220-801 A+ Objective 2.3 Explain properties and characteristics of TCP/IP

39. Which statement about networks is correct?

A. A workgroup is a group of computers on a client/server network that are sharing resources.

B. A domain name identifies a network.

C. The process of associating a character-based name with an IP address is called network address translation.

D. A fully qualified host name (FQHN) identifies a computer and the network to which it belongs.

220-801 A+ Objective 2.4 Explain common TCP and UDP ports, protocols, and their purpose

40. What term describes the process of associating a character-based name with an IP address?

    A. Name resolution

    B. Port triggering

    C. Multicasting

    D. Name forwarding

    220-801 A+ Objective 2.4 Explain common TCP and UDP ports, protocols, and their purpose

41. For TCP to guarantee delivery, it must use network protocols to establish a session between client and server to verify that communication has taken place. What protocols are used for this purpose?

    A. FTP

    B. IP

    C. Telnet

    D. Ethernet

    220-801 A+ Objective 2.4 Explain common TCP and UDP ports, protocols, and their purpose

42. Which statement regarding data transmission is correct?

    A. Telnet transmissions are encrypted.

    B. HTTPS is used by web browsers and servers to encrypt the data before it is sent and then decrypt it before the data is processed.

    C. The POP3 protocol is used to send email to a recipient's mail server.

    D. Data sent and received using the LDAP protocol is encrypted.

    220-801 A+ Objective 2.4 Explain common TCP and UDP ports, protocols, and their purpose

43. Which statement regarding protocols is correct?

    A. FTP is the protocol used by Windows to share files and printers on a network.

    B. The Secure Shell (SSH) protocol is used to pass login information to a remote computer and control that computer over a network.

    C. Internet Message Access Protocol, version 4, is used by various client applications when the application needs to query a database.

    D. Secure FTP (SFTP) is used to monitor network traffic.

    220-801 A+ Objective 2.4 Explain common TCP and UDP ports, protocols, and their purpose

44. FTP clients receive data on which of the following ports?

    A. 20

    B. 21

    C. 22

    D. 23

    220-801 A+ Objective 2.4 Explain common TCP and UDP ports, protocols, and their purpose

45. A DNS server listens for requests on which of the following ports?

   A. 23

   B. 25

   C. 53

   D. 67

   220-801 A+ Objective 2.4 Explain common TCP and UDP ports, protocols, and their purpose

46. An email client using IMAP receives email on port _____.

   A. 110

   B. 143

   C. 443

   D. 3389

   220-801 A+ Objective 2.4 Explain common TCP and UDP ports, protocols, and their purpose

47. An email client using POP3 receives email on port _____.

   A. 80

   B. 110

   C. 143

   D. 443

   220-801 A+ Objective 2.4 Explain common TCP and UDP ports, protocols, and their purpose

48. Which statement regarding a SOHO router is correct?

   A. As a router, it stands between the ISP network and the local network, routing traffic between the two networks.

   B. As a DHCP server, it manages several network ports that can be connected to wired computers, or to a switch that provides more ports for more computers.

   C. As a switch, it blocks unwanted traffic initiated from the Internet and provides Network Address Translation (NAT) so that computers on the LAN can use private or link local IP addresses.

   D. As a DHCP server, you can connect an external hard drive to the router, and the FTP firmware on the router can be used to share files with network users.

   220-801 A+ Objective 2.6 Install, configure, and deploy a SOHO wireless/wired router using appropriate settings

2

49. Which statement regarding network speed and/or security is correct?

    A. The speed of a network depends on the speed of each device on the network and how well a router manages that traffic.

    B. Routers, switches, and network adapters currently run at three speeds: Gigabit Ethernet (1000 Gbps), Fast Ethernet (100 Kbps), or Ethernet (10 Kbps).

    C. It is impossible for anyone outside your building to gain access to your wireless access point, so there is no need to secure it.

    D. If your router is wireless, there is no need to change its password.

    220-801 A+ Objective 2.6 Install, configure, and deploy a SOHO wireless/wired router using appropriate settings

50. What process is used to open or close certain ports so that they can or cannot be used?

    A. Port forwarding

    B. Port triggering

    C. Port filtering

    D. Port casting

    220-801 A+ Objective 2.6 Install, configure, and deploy a SOHO wireless/wired router using appropriate settings

51. What process opens a port when a PC on the network initiates communication through another port?

    A. Port forwarding

    B. Port triggering

    C. Port filtering

    D. Port casting

    220-801 A+ Objective 2.6 Install, configure, and deploy a SOHO wireless/wired router using appropriate settings

52. When using port forwarding or port triggering, what should you keep in mind?

    A. You must lease a static IP address from your ISP so that people on the Internet can find you.

    B. If two computers on the network attempt to trigger the same port, the router will allow data to pass to either computer.

    C. For port forwarding to work, the computer on your network must have a dynamic IP address so that the router knows where to send the communication.

    D. For better security, port forwarding should be kept turned on.

    220-801 A+ Objective 2.6 Install, configure, and deploy a SOHO wireless/wired router using appropriate settings

53. If you are having problems getting port forwarding or port triggering to work, putting your computer in a(n) _____ can free it to receive any communication from the Internet.

A. DMZ

B. WWAN

C. Intranet

D. VPN

220-801 A+ Objective 2.6 Install, configure, and deploy a SOHO wireless/wired router using appropriate settings

54. What Wi-Fi standard has the following characteristics?

- Speeds up to 500 Mbps depending on the configuration
- Indoor range up to 70 meters and outdoor range up to 250 meters
- Can use either 5.0 GHz or 2.4 GHz radio frequency

A. IEEE 802.11a

B. IEEE 802.11b

C. IEEE 802.11g

D. IEEE 802.11n

220-801 A+ Objective 2.5 Compare and contrast wireless networking standards and encryption types

55. What Wi-Fi standard has the following characteristics?

- Speeds up to 11 Mbps with a range of up to 100 meters (Indoor ranges are less than outdoor ranges.)
- Interference from cordless phones and microwaves at the radio frequency of 2.4 GHz

A. IEEE 802.11a

B. IEEE 802.11b

C. IEEE 802.11g

D. IEEE 802.11n

220-801 A+ Objective 2.5 Compare and contrast wireless networking standards and encryption types

56. When configuring an 802.11n network, what should you keep in mind?

A. Use 5 GHz frequency if your hotspot must reach a longer distance.

B. Bandwidth is a specific radio frequency within a broader frequency.

C. If your network must support older 802.11 b/g wireless devices, you must support the 2.4 GHz frequency.

D. For a 5 GHz network, the choices are 40 MHz and 20 MHz channel widths. For less interference, use 40 MHz.

220-801 A+ Objective 2.5 Compare and contrast wireless networking standards and encryption types

57. Which statement regarding wireless encryption is correct?

    A. WEP (Wired Equivalent Privacy) is considered very secure because the key used for encryption is dynamic.

    B. WPA (Wi-Fi Protected Access) encryption is stronger than WEP and was designed to replace it.

    C. WPA4 (Wi-Fi Protected Access 4) is the latest and best wireless encryption standard. It is based on the AES (Advanced Encryption Standard).

    D. MAC address filtering is considered a strong security measure because it uses encryption.

    220-801 A+ Objective 2.5 Compare and contrast wireless networking standards and encryption types

58. What type of network covers a small local area such as a home, office, other building, or small group of buildings?

    A. PAN

    B. LAN

    C. MAN

    D. WAN

    220-801 A+ Objective 2.8 Identify various types of networks

59. What type of network covers a limited geographical area, and is popular in places where networking cables are difficult to install, such as outdoors, in public places, and in homes that are not wired for networks?

    A. PAN

    B. LAN

    C. MAN

    D. WLAN

    220-801 A+ Objective 2.8 Identify various types of networks

60. What type of network consists of personal devices communicating at close range, such as a cell phone and notebook computer?

    A. PAN

    B. LAN

    C. MAN

    D. WAN

    220-801 A+ Objective 2.8 Identify various types of networks

61. What term describes how the connections between computers are physically arranged?

    A. Network topology

    B. Network design

    C. Network architecture

    D. Network map

    220-801 A+ Objective 2.8 Identify various types of networks

62. Several wireless computers each set up their own ad hoc mode network. This group of networked computers is known as a _____.

    A. ring network

    B. bus network

    C. star network

    D. mesh network

    220-801 A+ Objective 2.8 Identify various types of networks

63. When a star network uses multiple switches in sequence, the switches form a bus network. What term describes this network topology?

    A. Ring network

    B. Hybrid network

    C. Fully connected mesh network

    D. Mesh network

    220-801 A+ Objective 2.8 Identify various types of networks

64. What network topology uses a centralized device to manage traffic on the network?

    A. Ring network

    B. Bus network

    C. Star network

    D. Mesh network

    220-801 A+ Objective 2.8 Identify various types of networks

65. Which statement regarding network connections is correct?

    A. By default, an ad hoc network is deleted after you, or all users, disconnect from the network.

    B. When connecting to an ISP, download speeds are generally slower than upload speeds.

    C. Network transmissions invariably experience delays, however this does not affect network performance.

    D. To connect to the Internet, a network first connects to a Telnet server.

    220-801 A+ Objective 2.8 Identify various types of networks

66. What term refers to the theoretical number of bits that can be transmitted over a network at one time, similar to the number of lanes on a highway?

    A. Bandwidth

    B. Data throughput

    C. Latency

    D. Broadband

    220-801 A+ Objective 2.7 Compare and contrast Internet connection types and features

67. What is measured by the round-trip time it takes for a data packet to travel from source to destination and back to source?

    A. Bandwidth

    B. Data throughput

    C. Latency

    D. Broadband

    220-801 A+ Objective 2.7 Compare and contrast Internet connection types and features

68. What is the maximum speed of the 2G EDGE or 2G E cellular technology?

    A. Up to 50 Kbps

    B. Up to 56 Kbps

    C. 64 Kbps or 128 Kbps

    D. Up to 230 Kbps

    220-801 A+ Objective 2.7 Compare and contrast Internet connection types and features

69. Which of the following uses either CDMA or GSM mobile phone services?

    A. ISDN

    B. 3G cellular

    C. Satellite

    D. Dial-up

    220-801 A+ Objective 2.7 Compare and contrast Internet connection types and features
    REF: 16-770

70. Which term refers to a networking technology that carries more than one type of signal, such as DSL and telephone, or cable Internet and TV?

    A. Broadband

    B. Latency

    C. Data throughput

    D. Bandwidth

    220-801 A+ Objective 2.7 Compare and contrast Internet connection types and features

71. What is the maximum speed of a T3 network?

    A. Up to 30 Mbps

    B. 44 Mbps

    C. Up to 20 Mbps upstream and 50 Mbps downstream

    D. Up to 52 Mbps

    220-801 A+ Objective 2.7 Compare and contrast Internet connection types and features

72. What type of network ranges up to six miles and is used to provide wireless access to an ISP in rural areas?

A. Wi-Fi 802.11g wireless

B. 802.11n wireless

C. Fast Ethernet (100BaseT)

D. 802.16 wireless (WiMAX) WiMAX 2.0

220-801 A+ Objective 2.7 Compare and contrast Internet connection types and features

73. What is the newest Ethernet standard that is expected to largely replace SONET, OC, and ATM because of its speed, simplicity, and lower cost?

A. Gigabit Ethernet (1000BaseT)

B. 802.11n wireless

C. 10-gigabit Ethernet (10GBaseT)

D. 802.16 wireless (WiMAX) WiMAX 2.0

220-801 A+ Objective 2.7 Compare and contrast Internet connection types and features

74. What technology uses ordinary copper phone lines and a range of frequencies on the copper wire that are not used by voice, thus making it possible to use the same phone line for voice and Internet at the same time?

A. CDMA

B. DSL

C. Wi-Fi

D. Cable Internet

220-801 A+ Objective 2.7 Compare and contrast Internet connection types and features

75. Which statement regarding connection technologies is correct?

A. Satellites require line-of-sight connectivity without obstruction from mountains, trees, and tall buildings.

B. Satellites do not usually experience delays in transmission.

C. WiMAX supports up to 105 Mbps with a range up to several miles and uses 2- to 11-GHz frequency.

D. WiMAX is defined under IEEE 802.11g.

220-801 A+ Objective 2.7 Compare and contrast Internet connection types and features

76. What is sometimes used as a last-mile solution for DSL and cable Internet technologies?

A. WiMAX

B. GSM

C. CDMA

D. Wi-Fi

220-801 A+ Objective 2.7 Compare and contrast Internet connection types and features

77. What is an open standard that uses digital communication of data, and is accepted and used worldwide?

    A. WiMAX

    B. CDMA

    C. GSM

    D. Wi-Fi

    220-801 A+ Objective 2.7 Compare and contrast Internet connection types and features

78. What type of network consists of cells, with each cell being controlled by a base station?

    A. WiMAX

    B. Cellular WAN

    C. Fiber-optic

    D. Satellite

    220-801 A+ Objective 2.7 Compare and contrast Internet connection types and features

79. What term refers to the ability to use your cell phone to browse the web, stream music and video, play online games, and use instant messaging and video conferencing?

    A. Wi-Fi

    B. CAT-5

    C. Power over Ethernet

    D. 2G, 3G, or 4G

    220-801 A+ Objective 2.7 Compare and contrast Internet connection types and features

80. A PC makes a direct connection to a local wired network via a(n) _____.

    A. network adapter

    B. NIC

    C. mesh network

    D. BNC connector

    220-801 A+ Objective 2.9 Compare and contrast network devices and their functions and their features

81. Which of the following is an example of a MAC address?

    A. 192.168.15.1

    B. 192.168.1.2 - 254

    C. 11-0C-6E-D

    D. 00-0C-6E-4E-AB-A5

    220-801 A+ Objective 2.9 Compare and contrast network devices and their functions and their features

82. A wired network adapter might provide indicator lights on the side of the RJ-45 port that indicate _____.

   A. the MAC address

   B. connectivity and activity

   C. support for Wake-on-LAN

   D. Power over Ethernet

   220-801 A+ Objective 2.9 Compare and contrast network devices and their functions and their features

2

83. Which of the following allows the adapter to wake up the computer when it receives certain communication on the network?

   A. Quality of Service

   B. Power over Ethernet

   C. Wake-on-LAN

   D. NIC

   220-801 A+ Objective 2.9 Compare and contrast network devices and their functions and their features

84. What network adapter feature provides the ability to control which applications have priority on the network?

   A. Quality of Service

   B. Power over Ethernet

   C. Wake-on-LAN

   D. Ethernet

   220-801 Objective 2.9 Compare and contrast network devices and their functions and their features

85. Suppose you need power for your webcam, but you are in a building without an electrical outlet nearby. What network adapter feature would be most helpful in this situation?

   A. Quality of Service

   B. Power over Ethernet

   C. Wake-on-LAN

   D. Half duplex transmission

   220-801 A+ Objective 2.2 Categorize characteristics of connectors and cabling

86. Which of the following is a type of twisted-pair cable that uses an RJ-11 connector?

   A. Switch

   B. Hub

   C. Modems

   D. Phone cords

   220-801 A+ Objective 2.1 Identify types of network cables and connectors

87. What term describes the two phone jacks that are included on modem cards in desktop computers?

A. RJ-11 jacks

B. RJ-25 jacks

C. RJ-45 jacks

D. RJ-51 jacks

220-801 A+ Objective 2.1 Identify types of network cables and connectors

88. Just before a packet is put on the network, the network adapter adds additional information to the beginning and end of the packet, and this information includes the source and destination MAC addresses. The packet with this additional information is called a _____.

A. switch

B. hub

C. frame

D. segment

220-801 A+ Objective 2.1 Identify types of network cables and connectors

89. What technology just allows for a pass-through and distribution point for every device connected to it, without regard for what kind of data is passing through and where the data might be going?

A. Switch

B. Hub

C. Crimper

D. Bridge

220-801 A+ Objective 2.9 Compare and contrast network devices, their functions, and features

90. How does a switch learn the MAC addresses of every device connected to it?

A. It learns this information as it receives frames and records the source MAC addresses in its MAC address table.

B. It learns this information as it receives signals.

C. It learns this information as it receives data from the wireless access point.

D. It learns this information as it receives data from the modem.

220-801 A+ Objective 2.9 Compare and contrast network devices, their functions, and features

91. What device stands between two segments of a network and manages network traffic between them?

A. Crimper

B. Switch

C. Hub

D. Bridge

220-801 A+ Objective 2.9 Compare and contrast network devices, their functions, and features

92. What is a TCP/IP protocol that manages voice communication over the Internet?

A. VoIP

B. NAS

C. Internet appliance

D. VPN

220-801 A+ Objective 2.9 Compare and contrast network devices, their functions, and features

93. Which of the following connects directly to a network by way of an Ethernet port or an embedded Ethernet cable?

A. VoIP phone

B. NAS

C. Internet appliance

D. Hub

220-801 A+ Objective 2.9 Compare and contrast network devices, their functions, and features

94. What device is an enclosure that provides multiple bays for hard drives and an Ethernet port to connect to the network, and is likely to support RAID?

A. VoIP phone

B. NAS

C. Internet appliance

D. Hub

220-801 A+ Objective 2.9 Compare and contrast network devices, their functions, and features

95. What device uses firmware to configure its TCP/IP settings (including its IP address) and the phone number assigned to it?

A. VoIP phone

B. Fiber optic phone

C. PAN phone

D. Hybrid phone

220-801 A+ Objective 2.9 Compare and contrast network devices, their functions, and features

96. What is a type of thin client designed to make it easy for a user to connect to the Internet, browse the web, use email, and perform other simple chores on the Internet?

A. VoIP phone

B. NAS

C. Internet appliance

D. Hub

220-801 A+ Objective 2.9 Compare and contrast network devices, their functions, and features

97. What is the maximum cable length of a 10Base2 (ThinNet) cable system?

    A. 100 meters or 328 feet

    B. 185 meters or 607 feet

    C. 500 meters or 1,640 feet

    D. Up to 2 kilometers (6,562 feet)

    220-801 A+ Objective 2.2 Categorize characteristics of connectors and cabling

98. What is the maximum cable length of a 10Base5 (ThickNet) cable system?

    A. 100 meters or 328 feet

    B. 185 meters or 607 feet

    C. 500 meters or 1,640 feet

    D. Up to 2 kilometers (6,562 feet)

    220-801 A+ Objective 2.2 Categorize characteristics of connectors and cabling

99. What is the maximum cable length of a 100BaseT (Fast Ethernet) cable system?

    A. 100 meters or 328 feet

    B. 185 meters or 607 feet

    C. 500 meters or 1,640 feet

    D. Up to 2 kilometers (6,562 feet)

    220-801 A+ Objective 2.2 Categorize characteristics of connectors and cabling

100. What cable system uses coaxial cable and an AUI 15-pin D-shaped connector?

    A. 10Base2 (ThinNet)

    B. 10Base5 (ThickNet)

    C. 100BaseT (Fast Ethernet)

    D. 100BaseFX

    220-801 A+ Objective 2.2 Categorize characteristics of connectors and cabling

101. What cable system uses twisted pair (UTP or STP) cable and an RJ-45 connector?

    A. 10Base2 (ThinNet)

    B. 10Base5 (ThickNet)

    C. 100BaseT (Fast Ethernet)

    D. 100BaseFX

    220-801 A+ Objective 2.2 Categorize characteristics of connectors and cabling

102. What cable system uses fiber-optic cable and ST or SC connectors or LC and MT-RJ connectors?

    A. 10Base2 (ThinNet)

    B. 10Base5 (ThickNet)

    C. 100BaseT (Fast Ethernet)

    D. 100BaseFX

    220-801 A+ Objective 2.2 Categorize characteristics of connectors and cabling

103. What is the maximum cable length of a 100BaseFL cable system?
    A. 100 meters or 328 feet
    B. 185 meters or 607 feet
    C. 500 meters or 1,640 feet
    D. Up to 2 kilometers (6,562 feet)
    220-801 A+ Objective 2.2 Categorize characteristics of connectors and cabling

104. Which statement regarding cabling is correct?
    A. Twisted pair cable comes in two varieties: unshielded twisted pair (UTP) cable and shielded twisted pair (STP) cable.
    B. Twisted-pair cable has three pairs of twisted wires for a total of six wires.
    C. CAT-6 has more crosstalk than CAT-5 or CAT-5e.
    D. You should never use CAT-5e or CAT-6 for Gigabit Ethernet.
    220-801 A+ Objective 2.2 Categorize characteristics of connectors and cabling

105. What type of cable uses a covering or shield around each pair of wires inside the cable that protects it from electromagnetic interference caused by electrical motors, transmitters, or high-tension lines?
    A. UTP cable
    B. STP cable
    C. Fiber-optic cable
    D. Coaxial cable
    220-801 A+ Objective 2.2 Categorize characteristics of connectors and cabling

106. What type of cable has a single copper wire down the middle and a braided shield around it?
    A. Coaxial cable
    B. Unshielded twisted-pair cable
    C. Fiber-optic cable
    D. Shielded twisted-pair cable
    220-801 A+ Objective 2.2 Categorize characteristics of connectors and cabling

107. What type of cable uses an F-connector?
    A. RG-59 coaxial cable
    B. Unshielded twisted-pair cable
    C. Fiber-optic cable
    D. RG-6 coaxial cable
    220-801 A+ Objective 2.2 Categorize characteristics of connectors and cabling

108. What type of cable transmits signals as pulses of light over glass or plastic strands inside protected tubing?
    A. Coaxial cable
    B. Unshielded twisted-pair cable
    C. Fiber-optic cable
    D. Shielded twisted-pair cable
    220-801 A+ Objective 2.2 Categorize characteristics of connectors and cabling

109. What type of connectors can fiber-optic cables use?

A. ST connectors only

B. ST, SC, LC, and MT-RJ connectors only

C. ST, SC, and MT-RJ connectors only

D. SC, LC, and MT-RJ connectors only

220-801 A+ Objective 2.2 Categorize characteristics of connectors and cabling

110. Which statement regarding Ethernet is correct?

A. 10-Gigabit Ethernet uses STP or UTP cabling rated CAT-5 or higher.

B. Two variations of 100BaseT are 100BaseTS and 100BaseFS.

C. Gigabit Ethernet is becoming the most popular choice for LAN technology.

D. 1000-Mbps Ethernet can be used on LANs, MANs, and WANs, and is also a good choice for backbone networks.

220-801 A+ Objective 2.2 Categorize characteristics of connectors and cabling

111. What tool can be used to test a network cable or port?

A. Loopback plug

B. Cable tester

C. Network multimeter

D. Toner probe

220-801 A+ Objective 2.10 Given a scenario, use appropriate networking tools

112. What tool can be used to locate the ends of a network cable in a building?

A. Loopback plug

B. Cable tester

C. Network multimeter

D. Toner probe

220-801 A+ Objective 2.10 Given a scenario, use appropriate networking tools

113. What tool can be used to detect Ethernet speed, duplex status, default router on the network, length of a cable, voltage levels of PoE, and other network statistics and details?

A. Loopback plug

B. Cable tester

C. Toner probe

D. Network multimeter

220-801 A+ Objective 2.10 Given a scenario, use appropriate networking tools

114. What is a two-part kit that is used to find cables in the walls of a building?

A. Loopback plug

B. Cable tester

C. Toner probe

D. Network multimeter

220-801 A+ Objective 2.10 Given a scenario, use appropriate networking tools

2

115. What tool can be used to build your own network cable or repair a cable?
A. Wire stripper
B. Punchdown tool
C. Crimper
D. Network multimeter
220-801 A+ Objective 2.10 Given a scenario, use appropriate networking tools

116. What tool is used to attach a terminator or connector to the end of a cable?
A. Wire stripper
B. Punchdown tool
C. Crimper
D. Network multimeter
220-801 A+ Objective 2.10 Given a scenario, use appropriate networking tools

117. What tool is used to punch individual wires in a network cable into their slots in the keystone RJ-45 jack that is used in an RJ-45 wall jack?
A. Wire stripper
B. Punchdown tool
C. Crimper
D. Network multimeter
220-801 A+ Objective 2.10 Given a scenario, use appropriate networking tools

118. What provides multiple network ports for cables that converge in one location such as an electrical closet or server room?
A. Patch panel
B. Keystone jack
C. Crimper
D. Patch cable
220-801 A+ Objective 2.1 Identify types of network cables and connectors

119. Which statement regarding cable connections is correct?
A. When terminating a cable in a keystone jack, you first gently push each wire down into the color-coded slot of the keystone jack and then you use the punchdown tool to punch the wire down all the way into the slot.
B. A straight-through cable has the transmit and receive lines reversed so that one device receives off the line to which the other device transmits.
C. Before the introduction of Gigabit Ethernet, 10BaseT and 100BaseT required that a straight-through cable be used to connect two like devices such as a switch to a switch.
D. A straight-through cable is used to connect two like devices such as a hub to a hub or a PC to a PC.
220-801 A+ Objective 2.10 Given a scenario, use appropriate networking tools

120. Which statement regarding cable wiring is correct?

   A. Twisted-pair cabling used with RJ-45 connectors is color-coded in six pairs.

   B. 10BaseT and 100BaseT Ethernet use four pins: pins 1 and 2 for receiving data and pins 3 and 6 for transmitting data.

   C. For Gigabit Ethernet (1000BaseT) that transmits data on all four pairs, you must not only cross the green and orange pairs but also cross the blue and brown pairs to make a cross-over cable.

   D. For 10BaseT and 100BaseT networks, if you use T568A wiring on one end of the cable and T568B on the other end of the cable, you have a straight-through cable.

   220-801 A+ Objective 2.1 Identify types of network cables and connectors

3.0

LAPTOPS

1. A(n) _____ is designed for portability and can be just as powerful as a desktop computer.

   A. iPad

   B. all-in-one computer

   C. notebook

   D. smartphone

   220-801 A+ Objective 3.3 Compare and contrast laptop features

2. A(n) _____ computer has the monitor and computer case built together and uses components that are common to both a notebook and a desktop computer.

   A. iPad

   B. all-in-one computer

   C. netbook

   D. smartphone

   220-801 A+ Objective 3.3 Compare and contrast laptop features

3. _____ can be voided by opening the case, removing part labels, installing other-vendor parts, upgrading the OS, or disassembling the system unless directly instructed to do so by the authorized service center help desk personnel.

   A. Warranties

   B. Copyrights

   C. Licenses

   D. Patents

   220-801 A+ Objective 3.3 Compare and contrast laptop features

4. A notebook _____ tells you how to use diagnostic tools, troubleshoot a notebook, and replace components.

   A. user manual

   B. hardware manual

   C. help manual

   D. service manual

   220-801 A+ Objective 3.3 Compare and contrast laptop features

5. _____ might contain directions for upgrading and replacing components that do not require disassembling the case, such as how to upgrade memory or install a new hard drive.

   A. User manuals

   B. Hardware manuals

   C. Help manuals

   D. Service manuals

   220-801 A+ Objective 3.3 Compare and contrast laptop features

6. Most notebook computers come with a(n) _____ on the hard drive that contains a copy of the OS build, device drivers, and preinstalled applications needed to restore the system to its factory state.

   A. extended partition

   B. system partition

   C. recovery partition

   D. disk partition

   220-801 A+ Objective 3.3 Compare and contrast laptop features

7. When you first become responsible for a notebook, make sure you have _____ containing the installed OS so that you can recover from a failed hard drive.

   A. software profiles

   B. hardware profiles

   C. device drivers

   D. recovery discs

   220-801 A+ Objective 3.3 Compare and contrast laptop features

8. What tip would you bear in mind when repairing or caring for a notebook?

   A. LCD panels on notebooks are fragile and can be damaged fairly easily.

   B. Always pick up or hold the notebook by the lid.

   C. Notebook computers tend to last as long as desktop computers.

   D. Placing heavy objects on top of the notebook case is generally considered harmless.

   220-801 A+ Objective 3.1 Install and configure laptop hardware and components

9. The _____ utility in Windows can be used to see a list of hard drives installed in a system and the partitions on each drive.

   A. Recovery

   B. Disk Management

   C. BIOS

   D. System

   220-801 A+ Objective 3.3 Compare and contrast laptop features

10. The _____ control the screen brightness on many notebooks.
    A. Shift key and F2 or F3
    B. Ctrl key and F3 or F7
    C. Alt key and F2 or F10
    D. Fn key and F5 or F6
    220-801 A+ Objective 3.3 Compare and contrast laptop features

11. The most common pointing device on a notebook is a _____.
    A. keyboard
    B. touchpad
    C. joystick
    D. mouse
    220-801 A+ Objective 3.1 Install and configure laptop hardware and components

12. IBM and Lenovo ThinkPad notebooks use a unique and popular pointing device embedded in the keyboard called a(n) _____.
    A. Express Card
    B. USB stick
    C. Stylus
    D. TrackPoint
    220-801 A+ Objective 3.1 Install and configure laptop hardware and components

13. Most peripheral devices on today's notebooks use a(n) _____ to connect to the notebook.
    A. USB port
    B. ExpressCard slot
    C. CardBus slot
    D. PC Card slot
    220-801 A+ Objective 3.1 Install and configure laptop hardware and components

14. A(n) _____ includes one or more variations of a PC Card, CardBus, and/or ExpressCard.
    A. PCMCIA card
    B. Mini PCI
    C. AC adapter
    D. ACPI
    220-801 A+ Objective 3.1 Install and configure laptop hardware and components

15. Three standards for PC Cards and PC Card slots that pertain to size are _____.
    A. Type A, Type B, and Type C
    B. Type A-1, Type A-2, and Type A-3
    C. Type I, Type II, and Type III
    D. Type B-1, Type B-2, and Type B-3
    220-801 A+ Objective 3.1 Install and configure laptop hardware and components

3

16. _____ improved PC Card slots by increasing the bus width to 32 bits, while maintaining backward compatibility with earlier standards.

   A. AC adapters

   B. CardBus slots

   C. Mini PCI slots

   D. eSATA ports

   220-801 A+ Objective 3.1 Install and configure laptop hardware and components

17. A(n) _____ is fully hot-pluggable (add a card while the system is on), hot-swappable (exchange or add a card while the system is on), and supports autoconfiguration.

   A. Mini PCI

   B. CardBus

   C. ExpressCard slot

   D. AC adapter

   220-801 A+ Objective 3.1 Install and configure laptop hardware and components

18. A(n) _____ is an electrical device that changes DC to AC and provides an outlet for your laptop's AC adapter.

   A. sheet battery

   B. docking port

   C. inverter

   D. port replicator

   220-801 A+ Objective 3.1 Install and configure laptop hardware and components

19. A(n) _____ attaches to the bottom of a notebook and adds up to six hours to the battery charge.

   A. sheet battery

   B. Lithium Ion

   C. inverter

   D. port replicator

   220-801 A+ Objective 3.1 Install and configure laptop hardware and components

20. If you are using the AC adapter to power your notebook when the power goes out, the installed battery serves as a built-in _____.

   A. surge protector

   B. power strip

   C. adapter

   D. UPS

   220-801 A+ Objective 3.1 Install and configure laptop hardware and components

21. _____ saves all work to the hard drive and powers down the system.
    A. Recovery mode
    B. Hibernation
    C. Sleep mode
    D. Standby mode
    220-801 A+ Objective 3.3 Compare and contrast laptop features

22. On the BIOS power screen, _____ state turns off the hard drive and monitor and keeps everything else running normally.
    A. S1
    B. S2
    C. S3
    D. S4
    220-801 A+ Objective 3.1 Install and configure laptop hardware and components

23. On the BIOS power screen, _____ state is referred to as sleep mode.
    A. S1
    B. S2
    C. S3
    D. S4
    220-801 A+ Objective 3.1 Install and configure laptop hardware and components

24. On the BIOS power screen, _____ state is referred to as hibernation.
    A. S2
    B. S3
    C. S4
    D. S5
    220-801 A+ Objective 3.1 Install and configure laptop hardware and components

25. On the BIOS power screen, _____ state is the power off state after a normal shutdown.
    A. S2
    B. S3
    C. S4
    D. S5
    220-801 A+ Objective 3.1 Install and configure laptop hardware and components

26. A(n) _____ provides ports to allow a notebook to easily connect to a full-sized monitor, keyboard, AC power adapter, and other peripheral devices.
    A. docking port
    B. port replicator
    C. inverter
    D. sheet battery
    220-801 A+ Objective 3.1 Install and configure laptop hardware and components

27. A(n) _____ provides the same functions as a port replicator but provides additional slots for adding secondary storage devices and expansion cards.

    A. docking station

    B. docking port

    C. inverter

    D. sheet battery

    220-801 A+ Objective 3.1 Install and configure laptop hardware and components

28. Some notebooks have a connector, called a(n) _____, on the bottom of the notebook to connect to a port replicator or docking station.

    A. sheet battery connector

    B. power interface

    C. inverter sheet

    D. docking port

    220-801 A+ Objective 3.1 Install and configure laptop hardware and components

29. A _____ is a group of settings, kept by Windows, about a specific hardware configuration.

    A. hardware profile

    B. port replicator

    C. recovery disc

    D. software profile

    220-801 A+ Objective 3.1 Install and configure laptop hardware and components

30. Before you send a notebook for repairs, if possible, _____ on the hard drive.

    A. back up any important data

    B. clear the cache

    C. erase the hard drive

    D. disable the firewall

    220-801 A+ Objective 3.1 Compare and contrast laptop features

31. What should you do before attempting to replace or upgrade a component installed in a notebook?

    A. Ground yourself by using an antistatic ground strap.

    B. Leave all ExpressCards, CDs, DVDs, flash memory cards, and USB devices inside the notebook.

    C. Make sure the AC adapter is connected to the computer and the electrical outlet.

    D. (1) If the notebook is attached to a port replicator or docking station, release it to undock the computer. (2) Insert the battery pack.

    220-801 A+ Objective 3.1 Compare and contrast laptop features

32. A 2.66" 204-pin SO-DIMM contains _____ memory.
    A. DDR3
    B. DDR2 SDRAM
    C. DDR SDRAM
    D. SDRAM
    220-801 A+ Objective 3.1 Compare and contrast laptop features

33. A 2.66" 200-pin SO-DIMM contains _____.
    A. DDR3
    B. DDR2 SDRAM
    C. DDR SDRAM
    D. SDRAM
    220-801 A+ Objective 3.1 Compare and contrast laptop features

34. A 2.66" 144-pin SO-DIMM contains _____.
    A. FPM or EDO
    B. DDR2 SDRAM
    C. DDR SDRAM
    D. SDRAM
    220-801 A+ Objective 3.1 Compare and contrast laptop features

35. A 2.35" 72-pin SO-DIMMs contains _____ memory.
    A. FPM or EDO
    B. DDR2 SDRAM
    C. Rambus
    D. SDRAM
    220-801 A+ Objective 3.1 Compare and contrast laptop features

36. A 160-pin SO-RIMM contains _____ memory.
    A. FPM or EDO
    B. DDR2 SDRAM
    C. Rambus
    D. SDRAM
    220-801 A+ Objective 3.1 Compare and contrast laptop features

37. Notebook IDE connectors use _____ pins.
    A. 10
    B. 40
    C. 44
    D. 50
    220-801 A+ Objective 3.1 Compare and contrast laptop features

38. For IDE drives, some notebooks use a(n) _____ to interface between the 44-pin IDE connector on the hard drive and a proprietary connector on the notebook motherboard.

    A. port replicator

    B. PC Card

    C. inverter

    D. adapter

    220-801 A+ Objective 3.1 Compare and contrast laptop features

39. When upgrading from a low-capacity drive to a higher-capacity drive, how would you transfer data from the old drive to the new one?

    A. Use an adapter.

    B. Use a USB-to-IDE port replicator .

    C. Use a USB-to-IDE or USB-to-SATA converter.

    D. Use an IDE-to-SATA converter.

    220-801 A+ Objective 3.1 Compare and contrast laptop features

40. Before deciding to replace a hard drive, _____.

    A. make sure you have the recovery media before you start

    B. disassemble the notebook

    C. make sure the AC adapter is plugged in

    D. insert the battery pack

    220-801 A+ Objective 3.1 Compare and contrast laptop features

41. Before opening the case of a notebook or touching sensitive components, you should always use a(n) _____ to protect the system against ESD.

    A. power strip

    B. ground strap

    C. AC adapter

    D. surge protector

    220-801 A+ Objective 3.1 Compare and contrast laptop features

42. When disassembling a notebook, and removing cables, know that sometimes cable connectors are _____ connectors, which require releasing the latch before removing the cable.

    A. PCI

    B. ESD

    C. USB

    D. ZIF

    220-801 A+ Objective 3.1 Compare and contrast laptop features

43. When reassembling a notebook, _____.

    A. make sure you tighten and overtighten all screws

    B. do it in the reverse order in which you disassembled it

    C. know that loose parts do not affect the functioning of the equipment

    D. do it in the same order in which you disassembled it

    220–801 A+ Objective 3.1 Compare and contrast laptop features

44. What steps would you take to remove the DVD drive from a typical notebook?

    A. (1) Remove the screw that holds the DVD drive to the notebook. (2) Slide the drive out of the bay. (3) Replace the screw.

    B. (1) Remove the screw that holds the DVD drive to the notebook. (2) Slide the drive out of the bay.

    C. (1) Remove the keyboard. (2) Remove the screw that holds the DVD drive to the notebook. (3) Slide the drive out of the bay. (4) Replace the screw.

    D. (1) Remove the keyboard. (2) Slide the drive out of the bay. (3) Replace the screw.

    220–801 A+ Objective 3.1 Compare and contrast laptop features

45. Mini PCI Express slots use _____ pins on the edge connector.

    A. 32

    B. 44

    C. 52

    D. 64

    220–801 A+ Objective 3.1 Compare and contrast laptop features

46. Mini PCI cards are about _____ the size of Mini PCI Express cards.

    A. half

    B. twice

    C. three times

    D. four times

    220–801 A+ Objective 3.1 Compare and contrast laptop features

47. What steps would you take to remove a full-size Mini PCIe card from a notebook?

    A. (1) Disconnect antenna (2) Remove screw (3)Pull and lift card from slot

    B. (1) Remove screw(2) Disconnect antenna (3)Pull and lift card from slot

    C. (1) Remove screw (2)Pull and lift card from slot

    D. (1) Remove screw (3) Lift card from slot

    220–801 A+ Objective 3.1 Compare and contrast laptop features

48. By far, the most used AMD mobile socket is the _____.

    A. ASB1

    B. AM2+

    C. PPGA988

    D. 638–pin S1 socket

    220–801 A+ Objective 3.1 Compare and contrast laptop features

3

49. For many laptops, removing the cover on the bottom of a laptop exposes the
_____.

A. CMOS battery

B. memory card

C. processor fan and heat sink assembly

D. motherboard

220-801 A+ Objective 3.1 Compare and contrast laptop features

50. _____ is expected to use only about 20 percent as much power as LCD
and gives better quality display than LCD.

A. LED

B. Plasma

C. CRT

D. OLED

220-801 A+ Objective 3.2 Compare and contrast the components within the display of a
laptop

4.0

PRINTERS

1. Windows can send the commands and data needed to build a page to the printer using a(n) _____.
   A. object-oriented language
   B. assembly language
   C. dataflow language
   D. PostScript language
   220-801 A+ Objective 4.1 Explain the differences between the various printer types and summarize the associated imaging process

2. _____ was developed by Hewlett-Packard and is considered a de facto standard in the printing industry.
   A. Printer Control Language
   B. PostScript language
   C. Java
   D. PHP
   220-801 A+ Objective 4.1 Explain the differences between the various printer types and summarize the associated imaging process

3. Windows 7/Vista uses either _____ for rendering based on the type of printer driver installed.
   A. HTML or XML
   B. GDI or HTML
   C. GDI or XPS
   D. XPS or XML
   220-801 A+ Objective 4.1 Explain the differences between the various printer types and summarize the associated imaging process

4. What is a bitmap?
   A. A type of electrophotographic printer
   B. A series of bits in rows and columns
   C. A printer language that competes with PostScript
   D. Text data that contains no graphics or embedded control characters
   220-801 A+ Objective 4.1 Explain the differences between the various printer types and summarize the associated imaging process

4

5. Each row in a bitmap is called a(n) _____.
   - A. raster line
   - B. interface
   - C. tractor feed
   - D. GDI

   220-801 A+ Objective 4.1 Explain the differences between the various printer types and summarize the associated imaging process

6. _____ draws and formats the page, converts it to bitmap form, then sends the almost-ready-to-print bitmap to the printer.
   - A. Java
   - B. PostScript
   - C. Printer Control Language
   - D. Graphics Device Interface

   220-801 A+ Objective 4.1 Explain the differences between the various printer types and summarize the associated imaging process

7. Text data that contains no graphics or embedded control characters is sent to the printer as is, and the printer can print it without any processing. This data is called _____.
   - A. qualitative data
   - B. tractor feed
   - C. raw data
   - D. continuous data

   220-801 A+ Objective 4.1 Explain the differences between the various printer types and summarize the associated imaging process

8. When buying a printer, which tip would you recommend?
   - A. For heavy business use, the best practice is to purchase a multi-purpose printer.
   - B. Routine maintenance and troubleshooting are easier and less expensive on single-purpose printers.
   - C. Inkjet printers require the interaction of mechanical, electrical, and optical technologies to work.
   - D. Routine maintenance and troubleshooting are more difficult and more expensive on single-purpose printers.

   220-801 A+ Objective 4.1 Explain the differences between the various printer types and summarize the associated imaging process

9. A(n) _____ is a type of electrophotographic printer that can range from a small, personal desktop model to a large, network printer capable of handling and printing large volumes continuously.
   - A. laser printer
   - B. ink jet printer
   - C. dot matrix printer
   - D. bubble jet printer

   220-801 A+ Objective 4.1 Explain the differences between the various printer types and summarize the associated imaging process

10. _____ require the interaction of mechanical, electrical, and optical technologies to work.

    A. Laser printers

    B. Ink jet printers

    C. Dot matrix printers

    D. Bubble jet printer

    220-801 A+ Objective 4.1 Explain the differences between the various printer types and summarize the associated imaging process

11. What are the seven steps of laser printing?

    A. (1) Charging or conditioning(2) Fusing (3) Processing the image (4) Exposing or writing (5) Developing (6) Transferring(7) Cleaning

    B. (1) Processing the image(2) Charging or conditioning(3) Fusing (4) Exposing or writing (5) Developing (6) Cleaning(7) Transferring

    C. (1) Processing the image (2) Charging or conditioning (3) Exposing or writing (4) Developing (5) Transferring (6) Fusing (7) Cleaning

    D. (1) Processing the image (2) Charging or conditioning (3) Fusing (4) Developing (5) Transferring(6) Cleaning(7) Exposing or writing

    220-801 A+ Objective 4.1 Explain the differences between the various printer types and summarize the associated imaging process

12. When laser printing, one bitmap image is produced for monochrome images. For color images, _____.

    A. one bitmap is produced for each of two colors

    B. two bitmaps are produced for each of four colors

    C. two bitmaps are produced for each of two colors

    D. one bitmap is produced for each of four colors

    220-801 A+ Objective 4.1 Explain the differences between the various printer types and summarize the associated imaging process

13. A laser printer can produce better quality printouts than a dot matrix printer, even when printing at the same dpi, because it can vary the size of the dots it prints, creating a sharp, clear image. What does Hewlett-Packard (HP) call this technology of varying the size of dots?

    A. TouchFlo technology

    B. Mini PCI Express

    C. PCMCIA technology

    D. REt (Resolution Enhancement technology)

    220-801 A+ Objective 4.1 Explain the differences between the various printer types and summarize the associated imaging process

14. When laser printing, the _____ uses heat and pressure to fuse the toner to the paper.

    A. fuser assembly

    B. imaging drum

    C. pickup roller

    D. print head

    220-801 A+ Objective 4.1 Explain the differences between the various printer types and summarize the associated imaging process

15. What information should you bear in mind when fixing or maintaining a laser printer?

    A. For color laser printers, the writing process repeats six times.

    B. The toner cartridge needs replacing the most often, followed by the image drum, the fuser cartridge, and the transfer assembly, in that order.

    C. For color laser printers, each color uses the same image drum.

    D. The image drum needs replacing the most often, followed by the fuser cartridge, the toner cartridge, and the transfer assembly, in that order.

    220-801 A+ Objective 4.1 Explain the differences between the various printer types and summarize the associated imaging process

16. One laser printer part that might need replacing includes the _____ that pushes forward a sheet of paper from the paper tray.

    A. transfer belt

    B. separation pad

    C. pickup roller

    D. fuser assembly

    220-801 A+ Objective 4.1 Explain the differences between the various printer types and summarize the associated imaging process

17. On a laser printer, the _____ keeps more than one sheet of paper from moving forward.

    A. transfer belt

    B. separation pad

    C. pickup roller

    D. fuser assembly

    220-801 A+ Objective 4.1 Explain the differences between the various printer types and summarize the associated imaging process

18. A printer that is able to print on both sides of the paper is called a(n) _____ printer.

    A. double assembly

    B. duplex assembly

    C. assembly

    D. duplex

    220-801 A+ Objective 4.1 Explain the differences between the various printer types and summarize the associated imaging process

19. A(n) _____ printer uses a type of ink-dispersion printing and does not normally provide the high-quality resolution of laser printers.

A. dot matrix

B. inkjet

C. daisywheel

D. drum

220-801 A+ Objective 4.1 Explain the differences between the various printer types and summarize the associated imaging process

20. A(n) _____ printer uses a print head that moves across the paper, creating one line of the image with each pass.

A. dot matrix

B. inkjet

C. daisywheel

D. drum

220-801 A+ Objective 4.1 Explain the differences between the various printer types and summarize the associated imaging process

21. _____ printers use tubes of ink that have tiny resistors near the end of each tube.

A. Bubble jet

B. Laser

C. Dot matrix

D. Daisywheel

220-801 A+ Objective 4.1 Explain the differences between the various printer types and summarize the associated imaging process

22. A _____ moves the print head and ink cartridges across the paper using a belt to move the assembly and a stabilizing bar to control the movement.

A. transfer belt

B. separation pad

C. stepper motor

D. tractor feed

220-801 A+ Objective 4.1 Explain the differences between the various printer types and summarize the associated imaging process

23. _____ are the two primary techniques used to measure paper quality.

A. Weight and bitmap

B. Weight and brightness

C. Brightness and bitmap

D. Weight and size

220-801 A+ Objective 4.1 Explain the differences between the various printer types and summarize the associated imaging process

4

24. A(n) _____ creates a printed page by using some mechanism that touches or hits the paper.

A. laser printer

B. inkjet printer

C. thermal printer

D. impact printer

220-801 A+ Objective 4.1 Explain the differences between the various printer types and summarize the associated imaging process

25. _____ printers use continuous tractor feeds and fanfold paper (also called computer paper) rather than individual sheets of paper.

A. Laser

B. Impact

C. Inkjet

D. Thermal

220-801 A+ Objective 4.1 Explain the differences between the various printer types and summarize the associated imaging process

26. _____ printers use heat to create an image.

A. Laser

B. Impact

C. Inkjet

D. Thermal

220-801 A+ Objective 4.1 Explain the differences between the various printer types and summarize the associated imaging process

27. _____ printers are used to print receipts, bar code labels, clothing labels, or container labels.

A. Thermal transfer

B. Impact

C. Inkjet

D. Laser

220-801 A+ Objective 4.1 Explain the differences between the various printer types and summarize the associated imaging process

28. A(n) _____ printer connects directly to a computer by way of a USB port, parallel port, serial port, or wireless connection (Bluetooth, infrared, or Wi-Fi).

A. impact

B. network

C. local

D. thermal

220-801 A+ Objective 4.2 Given a scenario, install, and configure printers

29. A(n) _____ printer has an Ethernet port to connect directly to the network or uses Wi-Fi to connect to a wireless access point.
    A. impact
    B. network printer
    C. local printer
    D. thermal printer
    220-801 A+ Objective 4.2 Given a scenario, install, and configure printers.

30. A network printer is identified on the network by its _____.
    A. IP address
    B. MAC address
    C. routing number
    D. serial number
    220-801 A+ Objective 4.2 Given a scenario, install, and configure printers

31. How would you install a local USB printer?
    A. Disable firewalls and antivirus programs, plug it in printer, then use Control Panel to configure and install it.
    B. Plug it in then use Control Panel to configure and install.
    C. Turn on the printer and set it within range of the access point or computer.
    D. Plug it in and Windows 7/Vista installs the printer automatically.
    220-801 A+ Objective 4.2 Given a scenario, install, and configure printers

32. To know the IP address of a network printer, direct the printer to print a
    _____.
    A. test page
    B. configuration page
    C. system file
    D. hardware profile
    220-801 A+ Objective 4.2 Given a scenario, install, and configure printers

33. Use the _____ to find out if a 32-bit or 64-bit OS is installed.
    A. Devices and Printers menu
    B. Control Panel
    C. System window
    D. Document window
    220-801 A+ Objective 4.2 Given a scenario, install, and configure printers

34. Parallel ports, commonly used by older printers, transmit data in parallel, _____ bits at a time.

    A. two

    B. four

    C. six

    D. eight

    220-801 A+ Objective 4.2 Given a scenario, install, and configure printers

35. What are the three categories of parallel ports?

    A. Enhanced Parallel Port, Line Printer Port, and System Parallel Port

    B. Line Printer Port, Standard Parallel Port, and System Parallel Port

    C. Extended Capabilities Port, System Parallel Port, and Default Parallel Port

    D. Standard Parallel Port, Enhanced Parallel Port, and Extended Capabilities Port

    220-801 A+ Objective 4.2 Given a scenario, install, and configure printers

36. Which port transmits data in only one direction?

    A. Standard Parallel Port

    B. Enhanced Parallel Port

    C. Extended Capabilities Port

    D. Default Parallel Port

    220-801 A+ Objective 4.2 Given a scenario, install, and configure printers

37. Which port transmits data in both directions?

    A. Standard Parallel Port

    B. Enhanced Parallel Port

    C. Extended Capabilities Port

    D. Default Parallel Port

    220-801 A+ Objective 4.2 Given a scenario, install, and configure printers

38. A parallel cable has a DB25 connection at the PC end of the cable and a _____ connection at the printer end of the cable.

    A. 12-pin Centronics

    B. 16-pin Centronics

    C. 36-pin Centronics

    D. 44-pin Centronics

    220-801 A+ Objective 4.2 Given a scenario, install, and configure printers

39. Under what condition would remote users not be able to use a shared printer?

    A. If the printer is behind a firewall

    B. If the printer is connected to a network

    C. If the printer is asleep

    D. If the printer has an intrusion detection system installed

    220-801 A+ Objective 4.2 Given a scenario, install, and configure printers

40. Which method would you use to install a shared printer on a remote computer?
    A. Windows 7 Devices and Printers window
    B. Systems window
    C. Documents window
    D. BIOS setup window
    220-801 A+ Objective 4.2 Given a scenario, install, and configure printers

41. When print jobs accumulate in the queue, the process is called _____.
    A. imaging
    B. compiling
    C. tracking
    D. spooling
    220-801 A+ Objective 4.2 Given a scenario, install, and configure printers

42. How would you clean the inside of a printer?
    A. Use an ammonia-based cleaner.
    B. With a dry cloth, remove dust, bits of paper, and stray toner.
    C. Blow it out with compressed air.
    D. Use an antistatic vacuum cleaner.
    220-801 A+ Objective 4.3 Given a scenario, perform printer maintenance

43. A(n) _____ is a vacuum cleaner designed to pick up toner.
    A. extension magnet brush
    B. separation brush
    C. toner vacuum
    D. transfer brush
    220-801 A+ Objective 4.3 Given a scenario, perform printer maintenance

44. An inkjet printer might require _____ to align and/or clean the inkjet nozzles, which can solve a problem when colors appear streaked or out of alignment.
    A. calibration
    B. servicing
    C. repair
    D. realignment
    220-801 A+ Objective 4.3 Given a scenario, perform printer maintenance

45. Manufacturers of high-end printers provide _____, which include specific printer components, step-by-step instructions for performing maintenance, and any special tools or equipment that you need to do maintenance.
    A. printer realignment kits
    B. calibration kits
    C. printer maintenance kits
    D. hardware kits
    220-801 A+ Objective 4.3 Given a scenario, perform printer maintenance

4

46. After you have performed printer maintenance, be sure to _____ so that it will be accurate and will be able tell you when you need to do the next routine maintenance.

    A. calibrate the image drum

    B. realign the print head

    C. print a status report

    D. reset the page count

    220-801 A+ Objective 4.3 Given a scenario, perform printer maintenance

47. Suppose you are servicing the inside of an Oki Data color laser printer. As a last step, you should _____.

    A. plug in the printer

    B. carefully clean the LED erase lamps on the inside of the top cover

    C. remove the image drum from the printer

    D. dispose of the image drum

    220-801 A+ Objective 4.3 Given a scenario, perform printer maintenance

48. _____ can speed up memory performance, reduce print errors, and prevent "Out of Memory" errors.

    A. Extra memory

    B. Extra hard drives

    C. Less memory

    D. Fewer hard drives

    220-801 A+ Objective 4.3 Given a scenario, perform printer maintenance

49. A _____ is hardware or software that manages the print jobs sent to one or more printers on a network.

    A. print server

    B. print spooler

    C. duplex printer

    D. printer window

    220-801 A+ Objective 4.2 Given a scenario, install, and configure printers

50. A _____ can be: (1) A dedicated hardware device, (2) software, such as Print Queue Manager by AMT Software, which is installed on a computer on the network, or (3) programs embedded in firmware on a printer, such as HP JetDirect.

    A. print server

    B. duplex printer

    C. network printer

    D. print spooler

    220-801 A+ Objective 4.2 Given a scenario, install, and configure printers

5.0

OPERATIONAL PROCEDURES

1. A(n) _____ is a measure of electrical force.
   A. amp
   B. volt
   C. ohm
   D. joule
   220-801 A+ Objective 5.1 Given a scenario, use appropriate safety procedures

2. A(n) _____ is a measure of electrical current.
   A. amp
   B. volt
   C. ohm
   D. joule
   220-801 A+ Objective 5.1 Given a scenario, use appropriate safety procedures

3. A(n) _____ is a measure of resistance to electricity.
   A. amp
   B. volt
   C. ohm
   D. joule
   220-801 A+ Objective 5.1 Given a scenario, use appropriate safety procedures

4. A(n) _____ is a measure of work or energy.
   A. watt
   B. volt
   C. ohm
   D. joule
   220-801 A+ Objective 5.1 Given a scenario, use appropriate safety procedures

5. A(n) _____ is a measure of electrical power.
   A. watt
   B. volt
   C. ohm
   D. joule
   220-801 A+ Objective 5.1 Given a scenario, use appropriate safety procedures

5

6. _____ goes back and forth, or oscillates, rather than traveling in only one direction.

A. Alternating Current

B. A rectifier

C. Direct current

D. An inverter

220-801 A+ Objective 5.1 Given a scenario, use appropriate safety procedures

7. _____ travels in only one direction and is the type of current that most electronic devices require, including computers.

A. Alternating Current

B. A rectifier

C. Direct current

D. An inverter

220-801 A+ Objective 5.1 Given a scenario, use appropriate safety procedures

8. What device converts AC to DC?

A. Inverter

B. Rectifier

C. Direct current

D. Transformer

220-801 A+ Objective 5.1 Given a scenario, use appropriate safety procedures

9. What device converts DC to AC?

A. Inverter

B. Rectifier

C. Direct current

D. Transformer

220-801 A+ Objective 5.1 Given a scenario, use appropriate safety procedures

10. A(n) _____ is a device that changes the ratio of voltage to current.

A. inverter

B. rectifier

C. direct current

D. transformer

220-801 A+ Objective 5.1 Given a scenario, use appropriate safety procedures

11. _____ a line means that the line is connected directly to the earth, so that, in the event of a short, the electricity flows into the earth and not back to the power station.

A. Alternating

B. Grounding

C. Transforming

D. Inverting

220-801 A+ Objective 5.1 Given a scenario, use appropriate safety procedures

12. Which of the following is considered the easiest possible path for electricity to follow?

A. Ground

B. Capacitor

C. Inverter

D. UPS

220-801 A+ Objective 5.1 Given a scenario, use appropriate safety procedures

13. A(n) _____ holds its charge even after the power is turned off and the device is unplugged.

A. ground

B. capacitor

C. amp

D. inverter

220-801 A+ Objective 5.1 Given a scenario, use appropriate safety procedures

14. The power supply and monitor are both considered to be a(n) _____.

A. form factor

B. power supply tester

C. surge suppressor

D. field replaceable unit

220-801 A+ Objective 5.1 Given a scenario, use appropriate safety procedures

15. What advice would you give a technician who is concerned about putting out fires?

A. Class A extinguishers can put out fires caused by liquids such as gasoline, kerosene, and oil.

B. Water can be used to put out fires fueled by electricity.

C. Class A extinguishers can use water to put out fires caused by wood, paper, and other combustibles.

D. Class B fire extinguishers use nonconductive chemicals to put out a fire caused by electricity.

220-801 A+ Objective 5.1 Given a scenario, use appropriate safety procedures

5

16. Suppose you come indoors on a cold day, pick up a comb, and touch your hair. Sparks fly! What happened?

    A. Alternating current caused the sparks.

    B. Static electricity caused the sparks.

    C. Direct current electricity caused the sparks.

    D. Solar electricity caused the sparks.

    220-801 A+ Objective 5.1 Given a scenario, use appropriate safety procedures

17. Electrostatic discharge (ESD) can cause two types of damage in an electronic component: _____.

    A. major damage and upset damage

    B. upset damage and minor failure

    C. major failure and minor failure

    D. catastrophic failure and upset failure

    220-801 A+ Objective 5.1 Given a scenario, use appropriate safety procedures

18. Which device dissipates ESD and is commonly used by bench technicians who repair and assemble computers at their workbenches or in an assembly line?

    A. Ground bracelet

    B. Static shielding bag

    C. Ground mat

    D. Antistatic gloves

    220-801 A+ Objective 5.1 Given a scenario, use appropriate safety procedures

19. Which of the following rules can help protect computer parts against ESD?

    A. When passing a circuit board, memory module, or other sensitive component to another person, touch the other person before you pass the component.

    B. When unpacking hardware or software, leave the packing tape and cellophane in the work area. You might need them later.

    C. Always work on carpet.

    D. Do not work on a computer if you and/or the computer have just come in from the cold because there is more danger of ESD when the atmosphere is cold and dry.

    220-801 A+ Objective 5.1 Given a scenario, use appropriate safety procedures

20. A(n) _____ explains how to properly handle substances such as chemical solvents and how to dispose of them.

    A. Material Safety Data Sheet (MSDS)

    B. service manual

    C. motherboard manual

    D. user manual

    220-801 A+ Objective 5.2 Explain environmental impacts and the purpose of environmental controls

21. What are the steps involved in opening a computer case?

    A. (1) Power down the system and unplug it (2) Open the case cover

    B. (1) Back up important data (2) Power down the system and unplug it (3) Press and hold down the power button for a moment (4) Have a plastic bag or cup handy to hold screws (5) Open the case cover

    C. (1) Power down the system and unplug it (2) Have a plastic bag or cup handy to hold screws (3) Open the case cover

    D. (1) Back up important data (2) Power down the system and unplug it (3) Have a plastic bag or cup handy to hold screws (4) Open the case cover

    220-801 A+ Objective 5.1 Given a scenario, use appropriate safety procedures

22. What should you keep in mind when removing expansion cards?

    A. Place your fingers on the edge connectors.

    B. Stack the cards on top of one another.

    C. Lay each card aside on a flat surface.

    D. Remove the cards by rocking them from side to side.

    220-801 A+ Objective 5.1 Given a scenario, use appropriate safety procedures

23. On the front panel that connects to the motherboard, there are seven connectors. Which connector controls the drive activity light that lights up when any SATA or IDE device is in use?

    A. HDD LED

    B. Power SW

    C. Power LED+

    D. Reset SW

    220-801 A+ Objective 5.1 Given a scenario, use appropriate safety procedures

24. On the front panel that connects to the motherboard, there are seven connectors. Which connector controls power to the motherboard and must be connected for the PC to power up?

    A. HDD LED

    B. Power SW

    C. Power LED+

    D. Reset SW

    220-801 A+ Objective 5.1 Given a scenario, use appropriate safety procedures

25. On the front panel that connects to the motherboard, there are seven connectors. Which connector controls the power light and indicates that power is on?

    A. HDD LED

    B. Power SW

    C. Power LED+

    D. Reset SW

    220-801 A+ Objective 5.1 Given a scenario, use appropriate safety procedures

5

26. On the front panel that connects to the motherboard, there are seven connectors. Which connector controls the power light, in which the two positive and negative leads that indicate that power is on?

   A. Power LED–

   B. Power SW

   C. Power LED+

   D. Reset SW

   220-801 A+ Objective 5.1 Given a scenario, use appropriate safety procedures

27. On the front panel that connects to the motherboard, there are seven connectors. Which connector is the switch used to reboot the computer?

   A. Power LED–

   B. Power SW

   C. Power LED+

   D. Reset SW

   220-801 A+ Objective 5.1 Given a scenario, use appropriate safety procedures

28. _____ wires connecting the front panel to the motherboard are usually a solid color.

   A. Copper

   B. Negative

   C. Twisted pair

   D. Positive

   220-801 A+ Objective 5.1 Given a scenario, use appropriate safety procedures

29. _____ wires connecting the front panel to the motherboard are usually white or striped.

   A. Copper

   B. Negative

   C. Twisted

   D. Positive

   220-801 A+ Objective 5.1 Given a scenario, use appropriate safety procedures

30. Which technician is responsible for the PC before trouble occurs?

   A. Bench technician

   B. Technical retail associate

   C. PC service technician

   D. PC support technician

   220-801 A+ Objective 5.3 Given a scenario, demonstrate proper communication and professionalism

31. What software is designed and written to help solve problems and uses databases of known facts and rules to simulate human experts' reasoning and decision making?

    A. Motion control systems

    B. Neural networks

    C. Expert systems

    D. Data mining systems

    220-801 A+ Objective 5.3 Given a scenario, demonstrate proper communication and professionalism

32. When someone initiates a call for help, the technician starts the process by creating a(n) _____.

    A. pod

    B. ticket

    C. key

    D. record

    220-801 A+ Objective 5.3 Given a scenario, demonstrate proper communication and professionalism

33. A professional technician knows that it is his responsibility to set and meet expectations with a customer. How would you create an expectation of certainty?

    A. Establish a timeline with your customer for the completion of a project.

    B. Always make decisions for your customer.

    C. When explaining to the customer what needs to be done to fix a problem, do not offer repair or replacement options.

    D. When explaining to the customer what needs to be done to fix a problem, provide as little information as possible.

    220-801 A+ Objective 5.3 Given a scenario, demonstrate proper communication and professionalism

34. When working at a user's desk, which general guideline would you follow?

    A. If the user gets an important call while you are working, ask him to go somewhere else so as not to interfere with your work.

    B. If you are working on the printer and discover a budget report in the out tray, read it then hand it to the customer.

    C. Avoid distractions while you work.

    D. Always sit at the customer's desk chair.

    220-801 A+ Objective 5.3 Given a scenario, demonstrate proper communication and professionalism

5

35. As a help-desk technician, what would you do if you had a customer with very little computer knowledge?

    A. Be specific with your instructions. For example, instead of saying, "Open Windows Explorer," say, "Using your mouse, right-click the Start button and select Open Windows Explorer from the menu."

    B. Do not ask the customer to do something that might destroy settings or files without first having the customer back them up carefully. If you think the customer cannot handle your request, terminate the call.

    C. Do not encourage the customer to ask questions.

    D. If you determine that the customer cannot help you solve the problem without a lot of coaching, terminate the call.

    220-801 A+ Objective 5.3 Given a scenario, demonstrate proper communication and professionalism

36. As a help-desk technician, what would you do if you had a customer who was very proud of his computer knowledge?

    A. Let the customer know when she has made a mistake.

    B. When you can, compliment the customer's knowledge, experience, or insight.

    C. If the customer begins to use technical jargon, you should do the same.

    D. Speed up the conversation.

    220-801 A+ Objective 5.3 Given a scenario, demonstrate proper communication and professionalism

37. When someone purchases software from a software vendor, that person has only purchased a(n) _____ for the software, which is the right to use it.

    A. copyright

    B. trademark

    C. patent

    D. license

    220-801 A+ Objective 5.4 Explain the fundamentals of dealing with prohibited content/activity

38. _____ are intended to legally protect the intellectual property rights of organizations or individuals to creative works, which include books, images, and software.

    A. Patents

    B. Copyrights

    C. Trademarks

    D. Licenses

    220-801 A+ Objective 5.4 Explain the fundamentals of dealing with prohibited content/activity

39. The term _____ is used to describe the unauthorized copy of original software.

    A. software infringement

    B. social engineering

    C. patent infringement

    D. software piracy

    220-801 A+ Objective 5.4 Explain the fundamentals of dealing with prohibited content/activity

40. How can a company obtain the right to use multiple copies of software?

    A. By purchasing the patent

    B. By purchasing the copyright

    C. By purchasing a site license

    D. By purchasing the software

    220-801 A+ Objective 5.4 Explain the fundamentals of dealing with prohibited content/activity

41. What advice would you give a technician who needs to know how to physically protect a computer?

    A. Do not move or jar your desktop computer while the hard drive is working.

    B. Always set the tower case directly on thick carpet.

    C. Put face plates on expansion slot openings on the rear of the case.

    D. Put covers over the empty bays on the front of the case.

    220-801 A+ Objective 5.1 Given a scenario, use appropriate safety procedures

42. What advice would you give a technician who needs to know how to physically protect a computer?

    A. If your new laptop has just arrived and sat on your doorstep in freezing weather, bring it in immediately, unpack it, and turn it on.

    B. A server room where computers stay and people generally do not stay for long hours is set to balance what is good for the equipment and to conserve energy. High temperature and moderate humidity are best for the equipment.

    C. Leave the computer turned off for few weeks to give it a chance to rest.

    D. In BIOS setup, disable the ability to write to the boot sector of the hard drive.

    220-801 A+ Objective 5.1 Given a scenario, use appropriate safety procedures

5

43. A(n) _____ is a device that raises the voltage when it drops during brownouts or sags (temporary voltage reductions).

    A. power strip

    B. uninterruptible power supply

    C. adapter

    D. surge protector

    220-801 A+ Objective 5.1 Given a scenario, use appropriate safety procedures

44. A(n) _____ can be used as a surge protector to protect the system against power surges or spikes.

    A. power strip

    B. uninterruptible power supply

    C. adapter

    D. surge protector

    220-801 A+ Objective 5.1 Given a scenario, use appropriate safety procedures

45. A(n) _____ can provide power for a brief time during a total blackout long enough for you to save your work and shut down the system.

    A. power strip

    B. uninterruptible power supply

    C. adapter

    D. surge protector

    220-801 A+ Objective 5.2 Explain environmental impacts and the purpose of environmental controls

46. To completely wipe a hard drive clean without destroying it, you can use a(n) _____ downloaded from the hard drive manufacturer.

    A. zero-fill utility

    B. eraser utility

    C. cleaner utility

    D. degausser

    220-801 A+ Objective 5.2 Explain environmental impacts and the purpose of environmental controls

47. How would you dispose of alkaline batteries (AAA, AA, A, C, D, and 9-volt)?

    A. Dispose of them by returning them to the original dealer.

    B. Return these to the manufacturer or dealer to be recycled.

    C. Dispose of these batteries in the regular trash.

    D. Check with local county or environmental officials for laws and regulations in your area for proper disposal of these items.

    220-801 A+ Objective 5.2 Explain environmental impacts and the purpose of environmental controls

48. How would you dispose of button batteries used in digital cameras and other small equipment?

    A. Dispose of them by returning them to the original dealer or by taking them to a recycling center.

    B. Return these to the manufacturer or dealer to be recycled.

    C. Dispose of these batteries in the regular trash.

    D. Check with local county or environmental officials for laws and regulations in your area for proper disposal of these items.

    220-801 A+ Objective 5.2 Explain environmental impacts and the purpose of environmental controls

49. How would you dispose of ink-jet printer cartridges, computer cases, power supplies, and other computer parts?

    A. Dispose of them by returning them to the original dealer or by taking them to a recycling center.

    B. Do physical damage to the device so that it is not possible for sensitive data to be stolen.

    C. Dispose of these batteries in the regular trash.

    D. Check with local county or environmental officials for laws and regulations in your area for proper disposal of these items.

    220-801 A+ Objective 5.2 Explain environmental impacts and the purpose of environmental controls

5

50. How would you dispose of storage media such as hard drives, CDs, DVDs, and BDs?

    A. Dispose of them by returning them to the original dealer or by taking them to a recycling center.

    B. Do physical damage to the device so that it is not possible for sensitive data to be stolen.

    C. Dispose of these batteries in the regular trash.

    D. Check with local county or environmental officials for laws and regulations in your area for proper disposal of these items.

    220-801 A+ Objective 5.2 Explain environmental impacts and the purpose of environmental controls

Part II

CompTIA A+ Exam 220-802

1.0

OPERATING SYSTEMS

1. When two computers communicate using a local network or the Internet, communication happens at three levels. In addition to hardware and operating system, what is the third level?

   A. Protocol

   B. Driver

   C. Stack

   D. Application

   220-802 Objective 1.6: Setup and configure Windows networking on a client/desktop

2. What is the first step in in establishing communication between two computers using a local network or the Internet?

   A. One computer finds the other computer.

   B. Both computers agree on protocols.

   C. One computer becomes the server.

   D. Both computers agree on the rules for communication.

   220-802 Objective 1.6: Setup and configure Windows networking on a client/desktop

3. What is the communication model most commonly used between computers on a network or the Internet?

   A. Peer-to-peer

   B. Host-to-host

   C. Client/server

   D. Client/host

   220-802 Objective 1.6: Setup and configure Windows networking on a client/desktop

4. What is the suite of protocols used in almost all networks today?

   A. FTP

   B. TCP/IP

   C. IPX

   D. X.25

   220-802 Objective 1.6: Setup and configure Windows networking on a client/desktop

1

5. Before data is transmitted on a network, it is first broken up into segments. Each data segment is put into _____.

A. rows

B. headers

C. payloads

D. packets

220-802 Objective 1.6: Setup and configure Windows networking on a client/desktop

6. Besides the homegroup and workgroup, what is the third way in which Windows supports accessing resources on a network?

A. Sharegroup

B. Realm

C. Directory

D. Domain

220-802 Objective 1.6: Setup and configure Windows networking on a client/desktop

7. In Windows environments, a logical group of networked computers that share a centralized directory database of user account information and security for the entire group of computers is known as a _____.

A. domain

B. workgroup

C. homegroup

D. VLAN

220-802 Objective 1.6: Setup and configure Windows networking on a client/desktop

8. The four Ethernet speeds are 10 Mbps, 100 Mbps, 1 Gbps, and _____.

A. 2 Gbps

B. 5 Gbps

C. 10 Gbps

D. 100 Gbps

220-802 Objective 1.6: Setup and configure Windows networking on a client/desktop

9. The 48-bit identification number hard coded on every network adapter is known as the _____.

A. logical address

B. IP address

C. MAC address

D. network address

220-802 Objective 1.6: Setup and configure Windows networking on a client/desktop

10. What are the most popular client/server applications on the Internet?

    A. Telnet client and server

    B. FTP client and server

    C. E-mail client and server

    D. Web browser and server

    220-802 Objective 1.6: Setup and configure Windows networking on a client/desktop

11. What is the name of a small app or add-on that can be downloaded from a web site along with a web page and is executed by IE to enhance the web page?

    A. Extension

    B. Java Applet

    C. ActiveX control

    D. Javascript

    220-802 Objective 1.6: Setup and configure Windows networking on a client/desktop

12. Where in Internet Explorer can you block cookies from invading your privacy?

    A. Privacy tab

    B. Advanced tab

    C. Security tab

    D. Programs tab

    220-802 Objective 1.6: Setup and configure Windows networking on a client/desktop

13. A computer that intercepts requests that a browser makes of a server is known as a(n) _____.

    A. proxy server

    B. application gateway

    C. NAT server

    D. NAT filter

    220-802 Objective 1.6: Setup and configure Windows networking on a client/desktop

14. What is the initial screen that is displayed after the user logs on and Windows is loaded?

    A. Domain group

    B. Metro

    C. Aero

    D. Desktop

    220-802 Objective 1.1: Compare and contrast the features and requirements of various Microsoft Operating Systems

15. What is the name of Windows 7 3-D user interface?

    A. Domain group

    B. Aero user interface

    C. Metro user interface

    D. Desktop

    220-802 Objective 1.1: Compare and contrast the features and requirements of various Microsoft Operating Systems

16. Which version of Windows 7 has limited features and is available only in underdeveloped countries?

    A. Windows 7 Home Premium

    B. Windows 7 Starter

    C. Windows 7 Home Basic

    D. Windows 7 Limited

    220-802 Objective 1.1: Compare and contrast the features and requirements of various Microsoft Operating Systems

17. What is the simplest way to find out if a system can be upgraded to Windows 7?

    A. Download the Windows 7 Version Control.

    B. Connect to the Windows 7 Upgrade Assistant.

    C. Run the Windows 7 Upgrade Advisor.

    D. Check the Windows 7 Compatibility Center.

    220-802 Objective 1.1: Compare and contrast the features and requirements of various Microsoft Operating Systems

18. An extra copy of a data or software file that you can use if the original file becomes damaged or destroyed is also known as a(n) _____.

    A. cold copy

    B. hot copy

    C. backup copy

    D. external copy

    220-802 Objective 1.1: Compare and contrast the features and requirements of various Microsoft Operating Systems

19. What is the easiest and most reliable, but most expensive, backup solution for individuals and small organizations?

    A. Optical disks backup

    B. External hard drive backup

    C. Online backup

    D. Tape backup

    220-802 Objective 1.1: Compare and contrast the features and requirements of various Microsoft Operating Systems

20. What is the Windows utility that automatically backs up system files and stores them on the hard drive at regular intervals and just before you install software or hardware?

    A. Windows Backup Center

    B. Windows History Control

    C. Windows Restore Point

    D. Windows System Protection

    220–802 Objective 1.1: Compare and contrast the features and requirements of various Microsoft Operating Systems

21. Which of the following tools could be used to find out what processes are launched at startup and to temporarily disable a process from loading?

    A. Administrative Tools

    B. System Configuration

    C. Services Console

    D. Task Manager

    220–802 Objective 1.1: Compare and contrast the features and requirements of various Microsoft Operating Systems

22. Which of the following tools could be used to control the Windows and third-party services installed on a system?

    A. Administrative Tools

    B. System Configuration

    C. Services Console

    D. Task Manager

    220–802 Objective 1.1: Compare and contrast the features and requirements of various Microsoft Operating Systems

23. In Windows professional and business editions, a hard drive can be locked down by encrypting the entire Windows volume and any other volume on the drive using _____.

    A. Trusted Platform Module

    B. BitLocker Encryption

    C. USB User Authentication

    D. FileVault

    220–802 Objective 1.1: Compare and contrast the features and requirements of various Microsoft Operating Systems

24. What is the name of the antispyware included in Windows 7/Vista?

    A. Windows Defender

    B. Windows One

    C. Windows Security Suite

    D. Windows Premium Protection

    220–802 Objective 1.1: Compare and contrast the features and requirements of various Microsoft Operating Systems

1

25. What can be used in Windows Vista to confirm Windows Firewall, Windows Update, anti-malware settings?

    A. Administrative Tools

    B. Security Center

    C. Services Console

    D. Windows Defender

    220-802 Objective 1.1: Compare and contrast the features and requirements of various Microsoft Operating Systems

26. Reinstalling from which of the following is much faster than going through the detailed process of removing malware from a system?

    A. USB Flash drive

    B. Standard hard drive image

    C. Development backup image

    D. Restore backing image

    220-802 Objective 1.1: Compare and contrast the features and requirements of various Microsoft Operating Systems

27. Which version of Windows 7 includes BitLocker Drive Encryption?

    A. Windows 7 Professional

    B. Windows 7 Home Basic

    C. Windows 7 Enterprise

    D. Windows 7 Premium

    220-802 Objective 1.2: Given a scenario, install, and configure the operating system using the most appropriate method

28. Which of the following features is included in Windows 7 Home Basic?

    A. Aero user interface

    B. Scheduled backups

    C. Windows DVD Maker

    D. Windows XP Mode

    220-802 Objective 1.2: Given a scenario, install, and configure the operating system using the most appropriate method

29. Which of the following Windows 7 editions support multiple languages?

    A. Windows 7 Starter

    B. Windows 7 Home Premium

    C. Windows 7 Professional

    D. Windows 7 Ultimate

    220-802 Objective 1.2: Given a scenario, install, and configure the operating system using the most appropriate method

30. Which of the following Windows 7 editions support Windows XP Mode?

   A. Windows 7 Starter

   B. Windows 7 Professional

   C. Windows 7 Home Basic

   D. Windows 7 Home Premium

   220-802 Objective 1.2: Given a scenario, install, and configure the operating system using the most appropriate method

31. Which of the following Windows 7 license types can only be installed on a new PC for resale?

   A. Bundle license

   B. Retail license

   C. OEM license

   D. Starter license

   220-802 Objective 1.2: Given a scenario, install, and configure the operating system using the most appropriate method

32. What is the maximum memory supported by the 32-bit version of Windows 7 Home Basic?

   A. 2 GB

   B. 4 GB

   C. 8 GB

   D. 16 GB

   220-802 Objective 1.2: Given a scenario, install, and configure the operating system using the most appropriate method

33. Hard drive sectors are sometimes called _____.

   A. fields

   B. records

   C. frames

   D. cells

   220-802 Objective 1.2: Given a scenario, install, and configure the operating system using the most appropriate method

34. What is the name of the process used by hard drive manufactures for marking sectors?

   A. Low-level formatting

   B. High-level formatting

   C. Low-level marking

   D. High-level marking

   220-802 Objective 1.2: Given a scenario, install, and configure the operating system using the most appropriate method

1

35. Which of the following is roughly equivalent to one trillion bytes?

A. Megabyte

B. Gigabyte

C. Terabyte

D. Petabyte

220-802 Objective 1.2: Given a scenario, install, and configure the operating system using the most appropriate method

36. For magnetic hard drives, each platter is divided into concentric circles called _____.

A. rings

B. records

C. tracks

D. sectors

220-802 Objective 1.2: Given a scenario, install, and configure the operating system using the most appropriate method

37. What is the name of the sector where Windows stores the partition table?

A. Partition Sector

B. Master Boot Record

C. Definition Record

D. Mapping Sector

220-802 Objective 1.2: Given a scenario, install, and configure the operating system using the most appropriate method

38. Primary partitions are also called _____.

A. records

B. volumes

C. tracks

D. logical drives

220-802 Objective 1.2: Given a scenario, install, and configure the operating system using the most appropriate method

39. What is the name of the bootable partition that the startup BIOS turns to when searching for an operating system to start up?

A. Boot partition

B. Active partition

C. System partition

D. Master partition

220-802 Objective 1.2: Given a scenario, install, and configure the operating system using the most appropriate method

40. What are the two levels of command prompt windows supported by Windows 7 and Vista?

    A. Standard window and user window

    B. User window and administrator window

    C. Standard window and elevated window

    D. User window and privilege window

    220-802 Objective 1.2: Given a scenario, install, and configure the operating system using the most appropriate method

41. When working in the Command Prompt window, which command will clear the window?

    A. new

    B. erase

    C. clear

    D. cls

    220-802 Objective 1.2: Given a scenario, install, and configure the operating system using the most appropriate method

42. When working in the Command Prompt window, how can you retrieve the last command entered?

    A. Press the up arrow

    B. Press the down arrow

    C. Press Home

    D. Press Page Up

    220-802 Objective 1.2: Given a scenario, install, and configure the operating system using the most appropriate method

43. When working in the Command Prompt window, how can you terminate a command before it is finished?

    A. Press Ctrl+Insert

    B. Press Ctrl+Delete

    C. Press Ctrl+Pause

    D. Press Alt+Tab

    220-802 Objective 1.3: Given a scenario, use appropriate command line tools

44. Which tool protects system files and keeps a cache of current system files in case it needs to refresh a damaged file?

    A. File Manager

    B. System File Checker

    C. Disk Recover

    D. Disk Checker

    220-802 Objective 1.3: Given a scenario, use appropriate command line tools

45. Which tool is used in Windows to kill locked up or non-responding applications?

    A. System File Checker

    B. Event Manager

    C. Scheduler

    D. Task Manager

    220-802 Objective 1.3: Given a scenario, use appropriate command line tools

46. What is the name of the number that identifies each running process?

    A. Process code

    B. Process system number (PSN)

    C. Process number

    D. Process identify (PID)

    220-802 Objective 1.3: Given a scenario, use appropriate command line tools

47. Which Windows command can be used to manage hard drives, partitions, and volumes?

    A. diskpart

    B. chkdsk

    C. fdisk

    D. drivechk

    220-802 Objective 1.3: Given a scenario, use appropriate command line tools

48. Which diskpart command lists installed hard disk drives?

    A. select disk

    B. list partition

    C. list disk

    D. select partition

    220-802 Objective 1.3: Given a scenario, use appropriate command line tools

49. Which diskpart command removes any partition or volume information from the selected disk?

    A. erase

    B. remove

    C. clean

    D. format

    220-802 Objective 1.3: Given a scenario, use appropriate command line tools

50. Which diskpart command makes the selected partition the active partition?

    A. assign

    B. create partition primary

    C. select partition

    D. active

    220-802 Objective 1.3: Given a scenario, use appropriate command line tools

51. Which command tests connectivity by sending an echo request to a remote computer?

A. net use

B. ipconfig

C. ping

D. tracert

220-802 Objective 1.3: Given a scenario, use appropriate command line tools

52. Which command can display TCP/IP configuration information and refresh the TCP/IP assignments to a connection including its IP address?

A. net use

B. ipconfig

C. ping

D. tracert

220-802 Objective 1.3: Given a scenario, use appropriate command line tools

53. You can look for a program file or command by clicking on the Start button and entering the name in a box. In Vista, the box is labeled the _____ box, and in Windows XP, it is labeled the _____ box.

A. Search; Run

B. Run; Search

C. Find; Search

D. Search; Find

220-802 Objective 1.4: Given a scenario, use appropriate operating system features and tools

54. In Windows, a clickable item on the desktop that points to a program you can execute, or to a file or folder is called a _____.

A. trigger icon

B. desktop icon

C. program icon

D. shortcut icon

220-802 Objective 1.4: Given a scenario, use appropriate operating system features and tools

55. If Windows detects a problem while installing a device, it automatically launches the _____.

A. Help Center

B. Action Center

C. Device Manager

D. System Checker

220-802 Objective 1.4: Given a scenario, use appropriate operating system features and tools

1

56. What is the program file name for Windows Device Manager?
    A. devmgmt.exe
    B. device.exe
    C. devmgmt.msc
    D. sysmgmt.msc
    220-802 Objective 1.4: Given a scenario, use appropriate operating system features and tools

57. Video cards have their own processor. What is this processor called?
    A. Graphics renderer unit
    B. Video card accelerator
    C. Graphics processing unit
    D. Video processing unit
    220-802 Objective 1.4: Given a scenario, use appropriate operating system features and tools

58. The graphics processing unit is also known as a _____.
    A. graphics renderer unit
    B. video card accelerator
    C. visual processing unit
    D. video processing unit
    220-802 Objective 1.4: Given a scenario, use appropriate operating system features and tools

59. What is the primary tool for managing hard drives in Windows?
    A. File System Checker
    B. Device Management
    C. Disk Management
    D. Control Panel
    220-802 Objective 1.4: Given a scenario, use appropriate operating system features and tools

60. What is the program file name for Windows Disk Management?
    A. sysmgmt.msc
    B. diskmngr.exe
    C. devmgmt.msc
    D. diskmgmt.msc
    220-802 Objective 1.4: Given a scenario, use appropriate operating system features and tools

61. The portion of an OS that relates to the user and to applications is known as the
    _____.
    A. root
    B. shell
    C. kernel
    D. interface
    220-802 Objective 1.4: Given a scenario, use appropriate operating system features and tools

62. What part of the OS is responsible for interacting with hardware?

    A. root

    B. shell

    C. kernel

    D. interface

    220-802 Objective 1.4: Given a scenario, use appropriate operating system features and tools

63. You can quickly identify a problem with memory or eliminate memory as the source of a problem by using the Windows 7/Vista?

    A. Memory Management

    B. Memory Diagnostics

    C. System Diagnostics

    D. System Management

    220-802 Objective 1.4: Given a scenario, use appropriate operating system features and tools

64. What is the program file name for the Windows 7/Vista Memory Diagnostics?

    A. mdsched.exe

    B. memdgnst.msc

    C. memmgmt.msc

    D. sysmgmt.msc

    220-802 Objective 1.4: Given a scenario, use appropriate operating system features and tools

65. Which Windows tool gives a user access to a Windows desktop from anywhere on the Internet?

    A. Remote Session

    B. Remote Desktop

    C. Network Login

    D. Network Desktop

    220-802 Objective 1.4: Given a scenario, use appropriate operating system features and tools

66. To turn on the Remote Desktop service, open the System window and click _____.

    A. Advanced Settings

    B. Remote Settings

    C. System Protection

    D. Internet Options

    220-802 Objective 1.4: Given a scenario, use appropriate operating system features and tools

1

67. In addition to a hardware network firewall, a large corporation might use a software firewall, also called a _____.
    A. tier 2 firewall
    B. middleware firewall
    C. corporate firewall
    D. global firewall
    220-802 Objective 1.4: Given a scenario, use appropriate operating system features and tools

68. A personal firewall installed on a personal computer is also called a(n) _____.
    A. tier 1 firewall
    B. host firewall
    C. node firewall
    D. internal firewall
    220-802 Objective 1.4: Given a scenario, use appropriate operating system features and tools

69. The hardware or software that manages the print jobs sent to one or more printers on a network is known as a _____.
    A. print scheduler
    B. queue manager
    C. print manager
    D. print server
    220-802 Objective 1.4: Given a scenario, use appropriate operating system features and tools

70. Which version of Windows 7 offers the Print Management utility?
    A. Basic
    B. Starter
    C. Home Premium
    D. Professional
    220-802 Objective 1.4: Given a scenario, use appropriate operating system features and tools

71. Which of the following windows let you personalize the way Windows appears, including the desktop, sounds, mouse action, color themes, and display settings?
    A. Configuration
    B. Look and Feel
    C. Personalization
    D. Appearance
    220-802 Objective 1.5: Given a scenario, use Control Panel utilities (the items are organized by "classic view/large icons" in Windows)

72. The number of dots or pixels on the monitor screen expressed as two numbers such as 1680 × 1050 is known as the _____.

A. display level

B. screen resolution

C. screen size

D. display size

220-802 Objective 1.5: Given a scenario, use Control Panel utilities (the items are organized by "classic view/large icons" in Windows)

73. If you are installing an OEM version of Windows 7, look for a sticker on the outside of the DVD case. This sticker contains the product key and is called the _____.

A. OEM label

B. Certificate of Authenticity

C. Product certificate

D. Product label

220-802 Objective 1.5: Given a scenario, use Control Panel utilities (the items are organized by "classic view/large icons" in Windows)

74. If your computer is part of a Windows domain, when Windows starts up, it displays a blank screen instead of a logon screen. To display the logon screen and log onto the domain press _____.

A. Ctrl+Alt+Del

B. Alt+Tab

C. Ctrl+Esc

D. Ctrl+Alt+Esc

220-802 Objective 1.5: Given a scenario, use Control Panel utilities (the items are organized by "classic view/large icons" in Windows)

75. In order to make sure a valid Windows license has been purchased for each installation of Windows, Microsoft requires _____.

A. OEM activation

B. proof of authenticity

C. product activation

D. product certification

220-802 Objective 1.5: Given a scenario, use Control Panel utilities (the items are organized by "classic view/large icons" in Windows)

1

76. What is the name of a Microsoft software development tool that software developers can use to write multimedia applications such as games, video-editing software, and computer-aided design software?

A. WDDM

B. ActiveX

C. DirectX

D. GraphicsX

220-802 Objective 1.5: Given a scenario, use Control Panel utilities (the items are organized by "classic view/large icons" in Windows)

77. What Windows command could be used to display information about hardware and diagnose problems with DirectX?

A. wddm.exe

B. dxdiag.exe

C. dx.exe

D. dxgx.exe

220-802 Objective 1.5: Given a scenario, use Control Panel utilities (the items are organized by "classic view/large icons" in Windows)

78. What is the minimum video memory requirement for Windows to enable the Aero user interface?

A. 64 MB

B. 128 MB

C. 512 MB

D. 1 GB

220-802 Objective 1.5: Given a scenario, use Control Panel utilities (the items are organized by "classic view/large icons" in Windows)

79. The collection of user data and settings in Windows 7/Vista is known as a _____.

A. user namespace

B. user profile

C. user domain

D. user content

220-802 Objective 1.5: Given a scenario, use Control Panel utilities (the items are organized by "classic view/large icons" in Windows)

80. In general, what is a container to hold data, for example, a folder?

A. Profile

B. Domain

C. Namespace

D. Content

220-802 Objective 1.5: Given a scenario, use Control Panel utilities (the items are organized by "classic view/large icons" in Windows)

81. An Ethernet port is also known as a(n) _____.
    A. RJ-12 port
    B. DB9 port
    C. RS32 port
    D. RJ-45 port
    220-802 Objective 1.5: Given a scenario, use Control Panel utilities (the items are organized by "classic view/large icons" in Windows)

82. What is the name of the gateway a computer uses to access another network if it does not have a better option?
    A. Default gateway
    B. Network gateway
    C. Gateway server
    D. Central gateway
    220-802 Objective 1.5: Given a scenario, use Control Panel utilities (the items are organized by "classic view/large icons" in Windows)

83. A wireless network is created by a wireless device known as a _____.
    A. wired access point
    B. remote access point
    C. wireless access point
    D. wireless bridge
    220-802 Objective 1.5: Given a scenario, use Control Panel utilities (the items are organized by "classic view/large icons" in Windows)

84. Which protocols are used by some web servers to secure transmissions?
    A. SSH or RSA
    B. SSL or TLS
    C. DES or AES
    D. RSA or SSL
    220-802 Objective 1.5: Given a scenario, use Control Panel utilities (the items are organized by "classic view/large icons" in Windows)

85. Which box could be used to manage Internet Explorer settings?
    A. Internet Configuration
    B. Security Options
    C. IE Settings
    D. Internet Options
    220-802 Objective 1.5: Given a scenario, use Control Panel utilities (the items are organized by "classic view/large icons" in Windows)

1

86. If you want to delete your browsing history each time you close Internet Explorer, check "_____" on the General tab.

    A. Always delete temporary files on the General tab

    B. Always delete temporary files on the Security tab

    C. Delete browsing history on exit on the Security tab

    D. Delete browsing history on exit on the General tab

    220-802 Objective 1.5: Given a scenario, use Control Panel utilities (the items are organized by "classic view/large icons" in Windows)

87. If you need to configure Internet Explorer to use a specific proxy server, on the Connections tab, click _____.

    A. LAN settings

    B. Network settings

    C. Internet Options

    D. Internet settings

    220-802 Objective 1.5: Given a scenario, use Control Panel utilities (the items are organized by "classic view/large icons" in Windows)

88. In Vista, you can allow exceptions to Windows Firewall by program name or _____.

    A. file name

    B. process ID

    C. port number

    D. program extension

    220-802 Objective 1.5: Given a scenario, use Control Panel utilities (the items are organized by "classic view/large icons" in Windows)

89. Which is one of the best defenses against malware installing itself?

    A. Windows Update

    B. Windows Defender

    C. User Account Control box

    D. Administrator account

    220-802 Objective 1.5: Given a scenario, use Control Panel utilities (the items are organized by "classic view/large icons" in Windows)

90. Big Brother Professional is a type of _____.

    A. file manager system

    B. remote connection utility

    C. network manager tool

    D. network-monitoring software

    220-802 Objective 1.5: Given a scenario, use Control Panel utilities (the items are organized by "classic view/large icons" in Windows)

91. What is the most common pointing device on a notebook?
    A. TrackPoint
    B. Trackball
    C. Touchpad
    D. Pointing stick
    220–802 Objective 1.5: Given a scenario, use Control Panel utilities (the items are organized by "classic view/large icons" in Windows)

92. IBM and Lenovo ThinkPad notebooks use a unique and popular pointing device embedded in the keyboard called a _____.
    A. Touchpad
    B. TrackPoint
    C. Trackball
    D. Mouse ring
    220–802 Objective 1.5: Given a scenario, use Control Panel utilities (the items are organized by "classic view/large icons" in Windows)

93. As with all computer problems, begin troubleshooting by _____.
    A. interviewing the user
    B. turning the device off
    C. restarting the device
    D. unplugging the device
    220–802 Objective 1.5: Given a scenario, use Control Panel utilities (the items are organized by "classic view/large icons" in Windows)

94. To eliminate the printer as the problem, first check that the printer is on, and then _____.
    A. reset the printer
    B. install printer driver
    C. reboot the printer
    D. print a printer self-test page
    220–802 Objective 1.5: Given a scenario, use Control Panel utilities (the items are organized by "classic view/large icons" in Windows)

95. Which of the following is the primary Windows 7/Vista/XP tool for managing hardware?
    A. Control Panel
    B. Device Manager
    C. Action Center
    D. Action Manager
    220–802 Objective 1.7: Perform preventive maintenance procedures using appropriate tools

1

96. Which Windows utility could be used to disable or enable a device, update its drivers, uninstall a device, and undo a driver update?

    A. Control Panel

    B. Action Center

    C. Device Manager

    D. Action Manager

    220-802 Objective 1.7: Perform preventive maintenance procedures using appropriate tools

97. Besides Windows Updates and antivirus software, what is the third Windows setting critical for keeping the system protected from malware and hackers?

    A. IE Options

    B. Firewall

    C. Network location

    D. Security zones

    220-802 Objective 1.7: Perform preventive maintenance procedures using appropriate tools

98. What percentage of free space on the hard drive is needed by Windows for best performance?

    A. Less than 5 percent

    B. 10 percent

    C. About 15 percent

    D. More than 20 percent

    220-802 Objective 1.7: Perform preventive maintenance procedures using appropriate tools

99. The system image or Complete PC backup is a backup of the Windows volume and is called a _____.

    A. PC image

    B. volume image

    C. recovery image

    D. startup image

    220-802 Objective 1.7: Perform preventive maintenance procedures using appropriate tools

100. Which tool does Windows XP use to make a backup of the entire Windows volume?

    A. Backup Manager

    B. Recovery Center

    C. Action Center

    D. Automated System Recovery

    220-802 Objective 1.7: Perform preventive maintenance procedures using appropriate tools

101. To boot to the network, go into BIOS setup and set the first boot device to be Ethernet. The PC then boots to _____.

A. Network Boot Environment

B. Pre-Execution Environment

C. Ethernet Environment

D. Network Execution Environment

220-802 Objective 1.7: Perform preventive maintenance procedures using appropriate tools

102. The snapshots of the system created by the Windows System Protection are called _____.

A. backup points

B. rollback points

C. restore points

D. protection points

220-802 Objective 1.8: Explain the differences among basic OS security settings

103. To make sure System Protection has not been turned off, open the System window and click _____.

A. Backup options

B. System protection

C. Security options

D. Restore settings

220-802 Objective 1.8: Explain the differences among basic OS security settings

104. Where are restore points normally kept?

A. C:\System Volume Information

B. C:\Windows\system\backup

C. C:\System Restore Points

D. C:\Windows\System32\restore

220-802 Objective 1.8: Explain the differences among basic OS security settings

105. Which of the following options causes the host computer to turn on, even from a powered-off state, when a specific type of network activity happens?

A. Network Start

B. Wake on LAN

C. Network Boot

D. Pre-Execution State

220-802 Objective 1.8: Explain the differences among basic OS security settings

1

106. Wake on LAN must be supported by your motherboard and network adapter and must be enabled in both Windows and _____.

    A. Network Security options

    B. BIOS setup

    C. TCP/IP stack

    D. OS kernel

    220-802 Objective 1.8: Explain the differences among basic OS security settings

107. Which Windows utility, available with business and professional editions, controls what users can do with a system?

    A. System Permissions

    B. Access Control

    C. Group Policy

    D. System Policy

    220-802 Objective 1.8: Explain the differences among basic OS security settings

108. Which Windows utility, available with business and professional editions, could be used to set security policies to help secure a workstation?

    A. System Permissions

    B. Group Policy

    C. Access Control

    D. System Policy

    220-802 Objective 1.8: Explain the differences among basic OS security settings

109. What is used by personal computers to provide multiple virtual environments for applications?

    A. System session virtualization

    B. Desktop virtualization

    C. Server-side virtualization

    D. Client-side virtualization

    220-802 Objective 1.9: Explain the basics of client-side virtualization

110. Which of the following options allow a remote application running on a server to be controlled by a local computer?

    A. Application virtualization

    B. Client-side desktop virtualization

    C. Server-side desktop virtualization

    D. Presentation virtualization

    220-802 Objective 1.9: Explain the basics of client-side virtualization

111. Which of the following options could be used to create a virtual environment in memory for an application to virtually install itself?

    A. Server-side desktop virtualization

    B. Client-side desktop virtualization

    C. Application virtualization

    D. Presentation virtualization

    220-802 Objective 1.9: Explain the basics of client-side virtualization

112. Which of the following options allow software installed on a desktop or laptop to manage virtual machines?

    A. Server-side desktop virtualization

    B. Client-side desktop virtualization

    C. Application virtualization

    D. Presentation virtualization

    220-802 Objective 1.9: Explain the basics of client-side virtualization

113. Windows Virtual PC and Oracle VirtualBox are two examples of _____.

    A. Virtual machine clients

    B. Hypervisors

    C. Virtual machine servers

    D. Presentation virtualization software

    220-802 Objective 1.9: Explain the basics of client-side virtualization

114. Software used to create and manage virtual machines on a server or on a local computer is called _____.

    A. virtual machine manager

    B. virtual machine clients

    C. virtual machine servers

    D. presentation virtualization software

    220-802 Objective 1.9: Explain the basics of client-side virtualization

115. Which type of hypervisor installs on a computer before any operating system?

    A. Type 1

    B. Type 2

    C. Type 3

    D. Type 4

    220-802 Objective 1.9: Explain the basics of client-side virtualization

1

2.0

SECURITY

1. Which of the following options can improve network performance for an application by raising its priority for allotted network bandwidth?

   A. Firewall priority

   B. Quality of Service

   C. Network priority

   D. Quality of Connection

   220-802 Objective 2.1 Apply and use common prevention methods

2. To configure Windows to provide QoS for applications, you must enable QoS for the network connection and _____.

   A. firewall

   B. router

   C. scheduler

   D. adapter

   220-802 Objective 2.1 Apply and use common prevention methods

3. What is the program file name for the Group Policy console?

   A. grplcy.msc

   B. gpmgmt.msc

   C. gpedit.msc

   D. gpcntr.msc

   220-802 Objective 2.1 Apply and use common prevention methods

4. Group Policy works by making entries in the registry, applying scripts to Windows startup, shutdown, and logon processes, and affecting _____.

   A. security settings

   B. Internet settings

   C. network settings

   D. account settings

   220-802 Objective 2.1 Apply and use common prevention methods

2

5. Which types of policies are applied just before the logon screen appears?

   A. Site-based policies

   B. Account-based policies

   C. User-based policies

   D. Computer-based policies

   220-802 Objective 2.1 Apply and use common prevention methods

6. Which types of policies are applied after the logon screen appears?

   A. Account-based policies

   B. User-based policies

   C. Computer-based policies

   D. Domain-based policies

   220-802 Objective 2.1 Apply and use common prevention methods

7. When writing a policy, which of the following determines the priority level?

   A. Differentiated Services Code Point (DSCP) values

   B. Rule syntax

   C. Domain priority

   D. Domain scopes

   220-802 Objective 2.1 Apply and use common prevention methods

8. To apply a new policy, you can restart the computer or enter which of the following options at a command prompt?

   A. gpreboot.exe

   B. gprestart.exe

   C. gpupdate.exe

   D. gprefresh.exe

   220-802 Objective 2.1 Apply and use common prevention methods

9. In Windows, which of the following terms refers to the tasks an account is allowed to do in the system?

   A. Permissions

   B. Rights

   C. Roles

   D. Access

   220-802 Objective 2.1 Apply and use common prevention methods

10. In Windows, rights are also called _____.

    A. access

    B. roles

    C. permissions

    D. privileges

    220-802 Objective 2.1 Apply and use common prevention methods

11. In Windows, which of the following terms refers to which user accounts or user groups are allowed access to data files and folders?

A. Privileges

B. Rights

C. Permissions

D. Roles

220-802 Objective 2.1 Apply and use common prevention methods

12. Permissions are assigned to _____.

A. data files and folders

B. accounts

C. users

D. roles

220-802 Objective 2.1 Apply and use common prevention methods

13. Making sure the user account assigned to an employee has the required rights and no more is called the _____.

A. principle of least privilege

B. separation of duties

C. privilege escalation

D. privileges by roles principle

220-802 Objective 2.1 Apply and use common prevention methods

14. Using business and professional editions of Windows, user accounts can be assigned to different user groups using _____.

A. Access Control console

B. Group Policy console

C. User Account console

D. Computer Management console

220-802 Objective 2.1 Apply and use common prevention methods

15. Which type of Windows account has complete access to the system and can make changes that affect the security of the system and other users?

A. Standard

B. Administrator

C. Root

D. Supervisor

220-802 Objective 2.1 Apply and use common prevention methods

2

16. In Windows, a standard user account is also called a _____.
    A. restricted account
    B. regular account
    C. user account
    D. supervisor account
    220-802 Objective 2.1 Apply and use common prevention methods

17. Besides administrator, what other type of account does Windows XP offer for new accounts?
    A. Limited account
    B. Restricted account
    C. Supervisor account
    D. Standard account
    220-802 Objective 2.1 Apply and use common prevention methods

18. In Windows, to which group do administrator accounts belong by default?
    A. Supervisors group
    B. Users group
    C. Administrators group
    D. Managers group
    220-802 Objective 2.1 Apply and use common prevention methods

19. In Windows, to which group do standard user accounts belong by default?
    A. Supervisors group
    B. Users group
    C. Administrators group
    D. Managers group
    220-802 Objective 2.1 Apply and use common prevention methods

20. Which of the following Windows groups has limited rights on the system and is given a temporary profile that is deleted when the user logs off?
    A. Power Users group
    B. Backup Operators group
    C. Users group
    D. Guests group
    220-802 Objective 2.1 Apply and use common prevention methods

21. An account in which group can back up and restore any files on the system regardless of its access permissions to these files?
    A. Supervisors group
    B. Backup Operators group
    C. Power Users group
    D. Guests group
    220-802 Objective 2.1 Apply and use common prevention methods

22. Which of the following Windows XP groups can read from and write to parts of the system other than its own user profile folders, install applications, and perform limited administrative tasks?

A. Guests group

B. Supervisors group

C. Backup Operators group

D. Power Users group

220-802 Objective 2.1 Apply and use common prevention methods

23. Which group includes all user accounts that can access the system except the Guest account?

A. Everyone group

B. Authenticated Users group

C. Anonymous users group

D. Power Users group

220-802 Objective 2.1 Apply and use common prevention methods

24. When you share a file or folder on the network or to a homegroup, by default, Windows gives access to the _____.

A. Everyone group

B. Power Users group

C. Authenticated Users group

D. Anonymous Users group

220-802 Objective 2.1 Apply and use common prevention methods

25. Users who have not been authenticated on a remote computer are called _____.

A. Power users

B. Anonymous users

C. Operators

D. Blank users

220-802 Objective 2.1 Apply and use common prevention methods

26. What can you use on Windows business and professional editions to create your own user groups?

A. Management Console

B. Group Policy Console

C. Users Console

D. Roles console

220-802 Objective 2.1 Apply and use common prevention methods

2

27. When all users on a network require the same access to all resources, you can use a
_____.

    A. Domain homegroup

    B. Network account group

    C. Windows homegroup

    D. Shared Users group

    220-802 Objective 2.1 Apply and use common prevention methods

28. After the homegroup is set up, to share a file or folder with the homegroup, use the
_____.

    A. Domain Center

    B. Network Wizard

    C. Homegroup Console

    D. Sharing Wizard

    220-802 Objective 2.1 Apply and use common prevention methods

29. Which of the following methods lets you decide which users on the network have access to
which shared folder as well as the type of access they have?

    A. Network group sharing

    B. Homegroup sharing

    C. Domain controlling

    D. Workgroup sharing

    220-802 Objective 2.1 Apply and use common prevention methods

30. A computer dedicated to storing and serving up data files and folders is called a
_____.

    A. data server

    B. file server

    C. database

    D. content server

    220-802 Objective 2.1 Apply and use common prevention methods

31. In Windows 7, private data for individual users is best kept in which folder?

    A. C:\System\Users\Data

    B. C:\Documents and Settings

    C. C:\Users

    D. C:\System\Data

    220-802 Objective 2.1 Apply and use common prevention methods

32. Which folder is intended for folders and files that all users share?

    A. C:\Users\Public

    B. C:\System\Data\Public

    C. C:\Documents and Settings

    D. C:\System\Users\Public

    220-802 Objective 2.1 Apply and use common prevention methods

33. Using workgroup sharing, Windows offers two methods to share a folder over the network: share permissions and _____.

    A. network permissions

    B. NTFS permissions

    C. limited permissions

    D. restricted permissions

    220-802 Objective 2.1 Apply and use common prevention methods

34. Which of the following options grants permissions only to network users?

    A. Share permissions

    B. NTFS permissions

    C. Network permissions

    D. Domain permissions

    220-802 Objective 2.1 Apply and use common prevention methods

35. Besides NTFS and FAT32, which other type of volume supports Windows share permissions?

    A. ext2

    B. FAT16

    C. ext3

    D. exFAT

    220-802 Objective 2.1 Apply and use common prevention methods

36. Which of the following permissions apply to local users and network users and apply to both folders and individual files?

    A. Share permissions

    B. FAT permissions

    C. NTFS permissions

    D. FS permissions

    220-802 Objective 2.1 Apply and use common prevention methods

37. When permissions are passed from parent to child, it is called _____.

    A. parental permissions

    B. permission propagation

    C. inherited permissions

    D. top-down permissions

    220-802 Objective 2.1 Apply and use common prevention methods

2

38. Permissions that are attained from a parent object are called _____.

    A. parental permissions

    B. permission propagation

    C. inherited permissions

    D. top-down permissions

    220-802 Objective 2.1 Apply and use common prevention methods

39. Which Windows command can be used to change the rules for how inherited permissions are managed when copying and moving files?

    A. xcopy

    B. rcopy

    C. securecopy

    D. expertcopy

    220-802 Objective 2.1 Apply and use common prevention methods

40. When you move or copy an object to a folder, the object takes on the permissions of the _____.

    A. parent folder

    B. destination folder

    C. source folder

    D. default folder

    220-802 Objective 2.1 Apply and use common prevention methods

41. By default, when you share a folder in Windows XP, it is shared with everyone because XP uses _____.

    A. limited file sharing

    B. simple file sharing

    C. restricted access sharing

    D. network sharing

    220-802 Objective 2.1 Apply and use common prevention methods

42. Besides Client for Microsoft Networks, which other service is required by Windows XP to share resources?

    A. SMB Sharing

    B. File and Folder Sharing for LANs

    C. Data Sharing for Microsoft Networks

    D. File and Printer Sharing for Microsoft Networks

    220-802 Objective 2.1 Apply and use common prevention methods

43. Permissions that are manually set for a file or folder are called _____.
    A. local permissions
    B. manual permissions
    C. explicit permissions
    D. user permissions
    220-802 Objective 2.1 Apply and use common prevention methods

44. What Windows feature makes one computer (the client) appear to have a new hard drive, such as drive E, which is actually hard drive space on another host computer (the server)?
    A. Network drive map
    B. File and Printer sharing
    C. Client for Microsoft Networks
    D. File and Folder Sharing for Microsoft Networks
    220-802 Objective 2.1 Apply and use common prevention methods

45. Which device provides hard drive storage for computers on a network?
    A. Remote drive
    B. LAN-available drive
    C. Network-mapped storage device
    D. Network-attached storage device
    220-802 Objective 2.1 Apply and use common prevention methods

46. What makes it possible for files on the network to be accessed as easily as if they are stored on a local computer?
    A. Network Storage System (NSS)
    B. Network File System (NFS)
    C. NTFS
    D. Distributed Storage Protocol (DSP)
    220-802 Objective 2.1 Apply and use common prevention methods

47. If you want to share a folder, but don't want others to see the shared folder in Windows Explorer, add a $ to the end of the folder name. This type of folder is called a(n) _____.
    A. hidden share
    B. anonymous share
    C. private share
    D. limited share
    220-802 Objective 2.1 Apply and use common prevention methods

2

48. Folders and files on a computer that are shared with others on the network using local user accounts are called _____.
    A. regular shares
    B. standard shares
    C. local shares
    D. system shares
    220-802 Objective 2.1 Apply and use common prevention methods

49. Folders that are shared by default that administrator accounts at the domain level can access are called _____.
    A. system shares
    B. administrative shares
    C. supervisor shares
    D. domain shares
    220-802 Objective 2.1 Apply and use common prevention methods

50. The admin$ administrative share is called the _____.
    A. Administrator share
    B. System share
    C. Supervisor share
    D. Remote Admin share
    220-802 Objective 2.1 Apply and use common prevention methods

51. A user is _____ when he proves he is who he says he is.
    A. recognized
    B. identified
    C. authenticated
    D. authorized
    220-802 Objective 2.1 Apply and use common prevention methods

52. What is normally used by Windows to authenticate a user?
    A. Windows password
    B. Windows security token
    C. Digital certificate
    D. Public key
    220-802 Objective 2.1 Apply and use common prevention methods

53. A secure method for getting a logon window in Windows requires the user to press _____.
    A. Ctrl+Alt+Delete
    B. Ctrl+Insert+Home
    C. Ctrl+Esc
    D. Ctrl+Tab+Esc
    220-802 Objective 2.1 Apply and use common prevention methods

54. Which command can be used to change the way Windows logon works?

A. logonscrn

B. homescrn

C. winlogon

D. netplwiz

220-802 Objective 2.1 Apply and use common prevention methods

55. Generally speaking, which is the weakest link in setting up security in a computer environment?

A. Computers

B. People

C. Passwords

D. Protocols

220-802 Objective 2.2 Compare and contrast common security threats

56. The practice of tricking people into giving out private information or allowing unsafe programs into the network or computer is known as _____.

A. social manipulation

B. personal engineering

C. social engineering

D. people manipulation

220-802 Objective 2.2 Compare and contrast common security threats

57. The practice of peeking at a monitor screen when somebody else is working is called _____.

A. keylogging

B. eavesdropping

C. tailgating

D. shoulder surfing

220-802 Objective 2.2 Compare and contrast common security threats

58. Suppose someone who is unauthorized follows an employee through a secured entrance to a room or building. This is known as _____.

A. tailgating

B. mantrapping

C. shoulder surfing

D. shadowing

220-802 Objective 2.2 Compare and contrast common security threats

2

59. A user steps away from her computer and another person continues to use the Windows session because the system is not properly locked. This is known as _____.

    A. impersonation

    B. session hijacking

    C. tailgating

    D. shoulder surfing

    220-802 Objective 2.2 Compare and contrast common security threats

60. Which of the following options is a type of identity theft where the sender of an email message scams you into responding with personal data about yourself?

    A. Email hoax

    B. Phishing

    C. Spamming

    D. Pharming

    220-802 Objective 2.2 Compare and contrast common security threats

61. Any unwanted program that means you harm and is transmitted to your computer without your knowledge is called _____.

    A. grayware

    B. adware

    C. malicious software

    D. spyware

    220-802 Objective 2.2 Compare and contrast common security threats

62. Malicious software is also called _____.

    A. spyware

    B. grayware

    C. bloatware

    D. malware

    220-802 Objective 2.2 Compare and contrast common security threats

63. Any annoying and unwanted program that might or might not mean you harm is called _____.

    A. grayware

    B. whiteware

    C. adware

    D. scareware

    220-802 Objective 2.2 Compare and contrast common security threats

64. What is the term for a program that replicates by attaching itself to other programs?

A. Spyware

B. Virus

C. Worm

D. Trojan

220–802 Objective 2.2 Compare and contrast common security threats

65. A virus that hides in the MBR program in the boot sector of a hard drive or in an OS boot loader program is called a _____.

A. loading virus

B. BIOS virus

C. start virus

D. boot sector virus

220–802 Objective 2.2 Compare and contrast common security threats

66. Which type of software tracks all your keystrokes and can be used to steal a person's identity, credit card numbers, Social Security number, bank information, passwords, email addresses, and so forth?

A. Rootkit

B. Keylogger

C. Trojan

D. Spyware

220–802 Objective 2.2 Compare and contrast common security threats

67. Which type of software copies itself throughout a network or the Internet without a host program?

A. Worm

B. Trojan

C. Rootkit

D. Spyware

220–802 Objective 2.2 Compare and contrast common security threats

2

68. Which type of software does not need a host program to work but substitutes itself for a legitimate program?

A. Virus

B. Adware

C. Trojan

D. Rootkit

220–802 Objective 2.2 Compare and contrast common security threats

69. A type of virus that loads itself before the OS boot is complete is known as a
_____.

A. rootkit

B. boot sector virus

C. worm

D. Trojan

220-802 Objective 2.2 Compare and contrast common security threats

70. What is the quickest way to lock down a Windows workstation?

A. Press the power button on your computer.

B. Press the Windows key + L.

C. Press Ctrl+Esc.

D. Press Ctrl+Alt+Del.

220-802 Objective 2.3 Implement security best practices to secure a workstation

71. A password that is hard to guess by both humans and computer programs designed to hack passwords is called a _____.

A. one-time password

B. tokenized password

C. strong password

D. random password

220-802 Objective 2.3 Implement security best practices to secure a workstation

72. What is the minimum length of a password that is hard to guess by both humans and computer programs designed to hack passwords?

A. 5 characters

B. 6 characters

C. 8 characters

D. 12 characters

220-802 Objective 2.3 Implement security best practices to secure a workstation

73. Which tab of a policy Properties box will let read more about the policy and how it works?

A. Summary

B. Information

C. Details

D. Explain

220-802 Objective 2.3 Implement security best practices to secure a workstation

74. Which Windows command can be used to find out the resulting policies for the computer or user that are currently applied to the system?

    A. Gpset

    B. Gpresult

    C. Gpconsole

    D. Gptest

    220-802 Objective 2.3 Implement security best practices to secure a workstation

75. The group of policies in the Local Computer Policy, Computer Configuration, Windows Settings, Security Settings group can also be edited from the Control Panel. In the Control Panel, open the Administrative Tools and double-click _____.

    A. Local Security Policy

    B. Group Policy Console

    C. Computer Policy Tool

    D. Policy Configuration Utility

    220-802 Objective 2.3 Implement security best practices to secure a workstation

76. Which type of format can be used to overwrite the data on a drive with zeroes?

    A. Quick format

    B. High-level format

    C. Low-level format

    D. Fast format

    220-802 Objective 2.4 Given a scenario, use the appropriate data destruction/disposal method

77. Which device exposes a storage device to a strong magnetic field to completely erase the data on a magnetic hard drive or tape drive?

    A. Regausser

    B. Degausser

    C. ATA Secure Eraser

    D. EMP Eraser

    220-802 Objective 2.4 Given a scenario, use the appropriate data destruction/disposal method

78. What technique can be used to securely erase data from solid state devices such as USB flash drives or SSD drives?

    A. ATA Secure Eraser

    B. Regausser

    C. Degausser

    D. EMP Eraser

    220-802 Objective 2.4 Given a scenario, use the appropriate data destruction/disposal method

2

79. What is the best option for data destruction?

   A. ATA Secure Eraser

   B. Secure data-destruction service

   C. Degausser

   D. EMP Eraser

   220-802 Objective 2.4 Given a scenario, use the appropriate data destruction/disposal method

80. What is the best password policy regarding a SOHO router?

   A. Keep the password given to you by the cable company.

   B. Keep your e-mail password synced with the router password.

   C. Change the default password of your router firmware.

   D. Disable the router password when using antivirus software.

   220-802 Objective 2.5 Given a scenario, secure a SOHO wireless network

3.0

MOBILE DEVICES

1. Which of the following is an open source operating system that is based on the Linux OS and uses a Linux kernel?

   A. Symbian

   B. iOS

   C. Windows Phone

   D. Android

   220-802 A+ Objective 3.1 Explain the basic features of mobile operating systems

2. Which of the following is the name of a release of Android?

   A. Leopard

   B. Gingerbread

   C. Steel

   D. XP

   220-802 A+ Objective 3.1 Explain the basic features of mobile operating systems

3. On Android phones, up to four apps can be pinned to the _____, which is located at the bottom of the screen.

   A. dock

   B. menu bar

   C. Status bar

   D. taskbar

   220-802 A+ Objective 3.1 Explain the basic features of mobile operating systems

4. The official source for Android apps is _____.

   A. Android Shop

   B. Google Center

   C. Google Play

   D. Android Source

   220-802 A+ Objective 3.1 Explain the basic features of mobile operating systems

3

5. Most Android apps are written using the _____ programming language.

   A. Java

   B. JSP

   C. C++

   D. HTML

   220-802 A+ Objective 3.1 Explain the basic features of mobile operating systems

6. Apple iPhone and iPad both use the _____ operating system.

   A. Android

   B. Linux

   C. OS X

   D. iOS

   220-802 A+ Objective 3.1 Explain the basic features of mobile operating systems

7. Which of the following is true about the iOS?

   A. It is difficult to use.

   B. It is extremely stable.

   C. It has a number of bugs.

   D. It can only have up to six home screens.

   220-802 A+ Objective 3.1 Explain the basic features of mobile operating systems

8. Which of the following is true about iOS apps?

   A. They cannot be purchased individually.

   B. They can be distributed by any developer.

   C. They can only be downloaded from the iTunes App Store.

   D. They are distributed by Google.

   220-802 A+ Objective 3.1 Explain the basic features of mobile operating systems

9. An iOS app must be written in the _____ language.

   A. Java

   B. JavaScript or JSP

   C. Objective-C, C, or C++ programming

   D. HTML

   220-802 A+ Objective 3.1 Explain the basic features of mobile operating systems

10. A touch screen that can handle a two-finger pinch is called a _____ screen.

    A. spacer

    B. tracker

    C. multi-textual

    D. multitouch

    220-802 A+ Objective 3.4 Compare and contrast hardware differences in regards to tablets and laptops

11. The internal storage used by Android and iOS for their apps and data is a(n) _____, a type of flash memory.

A. USB

B. FRU

C. SSD

D. SIM

220-802 A+ Objective 3.4 Compare and contrast hardware differences in regards to tablets and laptops

12. A _____ is a device that contains a disc that is free to move and can respond to gravity as the device is moved.

A. gyroscope

B. GPS

C. Bluetooth

D. Wi-Fi

220-802 A+ Objective 3.4 Compare and contrast hardware differences in regards to tablets and laptops

13. A smartphone can determine its position by using _____ satellite data.

A. gyroscope

B. Bluetooth

C. GPS

D. VDI

220-802 A+ Objective 3.1 Explain the basic features of mobile operating systems.

14. A mobile device routinely reports its position to Apple or Google at least twice a day, and usually more often, which makes it possible for these companies to track your device's whereabouts. This is called _____.

A. geotracking

B. global positioning

C. trans-positioning

D. cell orientation

220-802 A+ Objective 3.1 Explain the basic features of mobile operating systems

15. Which of the following is used by the OS and apps of mobile devices to adjust the screen orientation from portrait to landscape as the user rotates the device?

A. Micro controller

B. Transformer

C. Grounder

D. Accelerometer

220-802 A+ Objective 3.1 Explain the basic features of mobile operating systems

3

16. Two devices being connected using Bluetooth might require a Bluetooth _____ to complete the Bluetooth connection.

    A. ID

    B. password

    C. PIN code

    D. pattern

    220-802 A+ Objective 3.2 Establish basic network connectivity and configure email

17. Email can be managed in two ways: using a browser, or using an email _____, such as Microsoft Outlook.

    A. client

    B. server

    C. host

    D. database

    220-802 A+ Objective 3.2 Establish basic network connectivity and configure email

18. Which protocol is used by the incoming server when you are managing your email on the server?

    A. POP

    B. HTML

    C. XML

    D. IMAP

    220-802 A+ Objective 3.2 Establish basic network connectivity and configure email

19. A POP server uses port _____ unless it is secured and using SSL.

    A. 110

    B. 993

    C. 995

    D. 8080

    220-802 A+ Objective 3.2 Establish basic network connectivity and configure email

20. By default, when using Gmail in iOS, you _____ a message that you no longer need rather than delete it.

    A. transfer

    B. archive

    C. purge

    D. compress

    220-802 A+ Objective 3.2 Establish basic network connectivity and configure email

21. For Apple devices, you can back up app data, iOS settings, email, contacts, wallpaper, and multimedia content, including photos, music, and videos, by syncing this content using iTunes or _____.

A. iArchive

B. iStore

C. iSync

D. iCloud

220-802 A+ Objective 3.5 Execute and configure mobile device synchronization

22. When you sync the content of Apple devices with iTunes, the backup is stored on your _____.

A. computer

B. iPhone

C. iOS

D. server

220-802 A+ Objective 3.5 Execute and configure mobile device synchronization

23. To configure iCloud on your Apple device with iOS 5 or higher, tap _____, and then iCloud.

A. Configure

B. Options

C. Home

D. Settings

220-802 A+ Objective 3.5 Execute and configure mobile device synchronization

24. To set a passcode on your iOS devices, tap _____, General, Passcode Lock, Turn Passcode On, and enter a four-digit code.

A. Security

B. Tools

C. Options

D. Settings

220-802 A+ Objective 3.3 Compare and contrast methods for securing mobile devices

25. For a lost mobile device, you can perform a _____, which remotely erases all contacts, email, photos, and other data from the device to protect your privacy.

A. auto-delete

B. remote wipe

C. remote protect

D. factory restore

220-802 A+ Objective 3.3 Compare and contrast methods for securing mobile devices

3

26. Which statement regarding mobile devices is correct?

    A. It is possible to upgrade internal components of mobile devices.

    B. Batteries of mobile devices cannot be replaced.

    C. There are no field-replaceable units (FRU) in mobile devices.

    D. SIM cards cannot be replaced.

    220-802 A+ Objective 3.4 Compare and contrast hardware differences in regards to tablets and laptops

27. Most of the settings you need to support an Android device are found in the _____ app.

    A. Settings

    B. Configure

    C. Tools

    D. Options

    220-802 A+ Objective 3.2 Establish basic network connectivity and configure email

28. On an Android device, restoring data and settings from backup can be a difficult process because _____.

    A. security settings established by Google are cumbersome

    B. Android devices do not allow any backups

    C. manufacturers pre-install apps to prevent backups

    D. no one app backs up all the data on an Android device

    220-802 A+ Objective 3.5 Execute and configure mobile device synchronization

29. For securing an Android device, you can set a(n) _____, PIN, or password that must be entered to unlock the device.

    A. graph

    B. pattern

    C. ID

    D. shape

    220-802 A+ Objective 3.3 Compare and contrast methods for securing mobile devices

30. _____ gives you complete access to the entire file system (all folders and files) and all commands and features of an Android device.

    A. Rooting

    B. Securing

    C. Controlling

    D. Targeting

    220-802 A+ Objective 3.3 Compare and contrast methods for securing mobile devices

4.0

TROUBLESHOOTING

1. What monitors the boot process and reports any errors that occur, usually as coded numbers on a small LED panel?

   A. Power supply tester

   B. POST card

   C. Loopback plug

   D. Crimper

   220-802 A+ Objective 4.2 Given a scenario, troubleshoot common problems related to motherboards, RAM, CPU and power with appropriate tools appropriate tools.

2. What is the first step of troubleshooting?

   A. Examine the system and make your best estimate.

   B. Plan your solution.

   C. Interview the user and back up data.

   D. Test your theory.

   220-802 A+ Objective 4.1 Given a scenario, explain the troubleshooting theory

3. In Windows, you might want to stop all nonessential services running in the background to eliminate them as a problem. This is part of the "_____" rule.

   A. try the simple things first

   B. divide and conquer

   C. beware of user error

   D. reboot and start over

   220-802 A+ Objective 4.1 Given a scenario, explain the troubleshooting theory

4. Good _____ helps you take what you learned into the next troubleshooting situation, train others, develop effective preventive maintenance plans, and satisfy any audits or customer or employer queries about your work.

   A. collaboration

   B. programming

   C. marketing

   D. documentation

   220-802 A+ Objective 4.1 Given a scenario, explain the troubleshooting theory

4

5. A _____ happens when processes running in kernel mode encounter a problem and Windows must stop the system.

   A. BSOD

   B. CODB

   C. DBE

   D. GIC

   220-802 A+ Objective 4.6 Given a scenario, troubleshoot operating system problems with appropriate tools

6. What is indicated by the NTFS_FILE_SYSTEM error?

   A. Volatile memory is bad.

   B. The application requires a patch.

   C. The processor requires a patch.

   D. The hard drive is most likely corrupted.

   220-802 A+ Objective 4.6 Given a scenario, troubleshoot operating system problems with appropriate tools

7. What is the immediate problem that causes the KERNEL_DATA_INPAGE_ERROR message?

   A. A user error

   B. An error with Windows reading the paging file (Pagefile.sys)

   C. An error with a specific application

   D. An error with Windows connecting to the network

   220-802 A+ Objective 4.6 Given a scenario, troubleshoot operating system problems with appropriate tools

8. What error is most likely caused by bad memory?

   A. DIVIDE_BY_ZERO_ERROR

   B. NTFS_FILE_SYSTEM

   C. UNEXPECTED_KERNEL_MODE_TRAP

   D. ERROR_NOT_DOS_DISK

   220-802 A+ Objective 4.6 Given a scenario, troubleshoot operating system problems with appropriate tools

9. What error is most likely to be caused by an application?

   A. DIVIDE_BY_ZERO_ERROR

   B. NTFS_FILE_SYSTEM

   C. UNEXPECTED_KERNEL_MODE_TRAP

   D. ERROR_NOT_DOS_DISK

   220-802 A+ Objective 4.6 Given a scenario, troubleshoot operating system problems with appropriate tools

10. The term x86 refers to _____-bit CPUs or processors and to _____-bit operating systems.
    A. 16
    B. 32
    C. 64
    D. 128
    220-802 A+ Objective 4.6 Given a scenario, troubleshoot operating system problems with appropriate tools

11. All CPUs installed in personal computers today are _____ processors.
    A. singular
    B. fluid
    C. bipolar
    D. hybrid
    220-802 A+ Objective 4.6 Given a scenario, troubleshoot operating system problems with appropriate tools

12. _____ protects system files and keeps a cache of current system files in case it needs to refresh a damaged file.
    A. Memory Diagnostics
    B. Fixmbr
    C. SFC
    D. Fixboot
    220-802 A+ Objective 4.6 Given a scenario, troubleshoot operating system problems with appropriate tools

13. Improper shutdowns and a system lockup that cause a computer to freeze and require that it be restarted are most likely caused by _____.
    A. hardware
    B. keyboards
    C. network errors
    D. application errors
    220-802 A+ Objective 4.6 Given a scenario, troubleshoot operating system problems with appropriate tools

14. If the system shuts down improperly, you can check _____ to see if it has reported a hardware failure.
    A. Safe Mode
    B. SFC
    C. Event Viewer
    D. Hardware Track
    220-802 A+ Objective 4.6 Given a scenario, troubleshoot operating system problems with appropriate tools

4

15. To boot to Safe Mode, press _____ before Windows loads.

    A. F2

    B. F4

    C. F5

    D. F8

    220-802 A+ Objective 4.6 Given a scenario, troubleshoot operating system problems with appropriate tools

16. For Windows 7, the _____ tracks problems with applications, hardware, and Windows.

    A. Action Center

    B. Windows Explorer

    C. Control Panel

    D. Start menu

    220-802 A+ Objective 4.6 Given a scenario, troubleshoot operating system problems with appropriate tools

17. When troubleshooting, the _____ logs might give clues about applications and the system.

    A. Windows Explorer

    B. Safe Mode

    C. Event Viewer

    D. Start menu

    220-802 A+ Objective 4.6 Given a scenario, troubleshoot operating system problems with appropriate tools

18. For essential hardware devices, use _____ to verify and replace system files.

    A. SFC

    B. System Restore

    C. Memory Diagnostics

    D. Task Manager

    220-802 A+ Objective 4.6 Given a scenario, troubleshoot operating system problems with appropriate tools

19. If you can identify the approximate date the error started and that date is in the recent past, use _____ to solve the problem.

    A. Task Manager

    B. SFC

    C. System Restore

    D. Windows Explorer

    220-802 A+ Objective 4.6 Given a scenario, troubleshoot operating system problems with appropriate tools

20. The _____ command uses the process ID to kill a process.
   A. Process Stop
   B. End Process
   C. End Task
   D. Taskkill
   220-802 A+ Objective 4.6 Given a scenario, troubleshoot operating system problems with appropriate tools

21. The file association between a data file and an application is determined by the _____.
   A. file extension
   B. file size
   C. association rule
   D. data structure
   220-802 A+ Objective 4.6 Given a scenario, troubleshoot operating system problems with appropriate tools

22. The _____ tool can be used to allow data files (called data sources) to be connected to applications they normally would not use.
   A. SFC
   B. Task Manager
   C. ODBC
   D. Windows Restore
   220-802 A+ Objective 4.6 Given a scenario, troubleshoot operating system problems with appropriate tools

23. What tool can be used to disable a service at startup?
   A. System Restore
   B. ODBC
   C. Disable Service
   D. System Configuration
   220-802 A+ Objective 4.6 Given a scenario, troubleshoot operating system problems with appropriate tools

24. When a service fails to start, you can use a service's _____ box in the Service console to find the path and filename to the executable program.
   A. Tools
   B. Properties
   C. File
   D. Options
   220-802 A+ Objective 4.6 Given a scenario, troubleshoot operating system problems with appropriate tools

4

25. If an application has never worked, you should try running the installation program or application as a(n) _____.

    A. administrator

    B. troubleshooter

    C. expert

    D. programmer

    220-802 A+ Objective 4.6 Given a scenario, troubleshoot operating system problems with appropriate tools

26. What verifies that the application is not a rogue application and that it is certified as Windows-compatible by Microsoft?

    A. File extension

    B. Encryption

    C. Watermark

    D. Digital signature

    220-802 A+ Objective 4.6 Given a scenario, troubleshoot operating system problems with appropriate tools

27. Which statement regarding user manuals is correct?

    A. User manuals are typically not helpful for problem-solving.

    B. The Internet does not provide any reliable information on solving computer problems.

    C. User manuals often list error messages and their meanings.

    D. A good PC technician should be able to solve problems without consulting user manuals.

    220-802 A+ Objective 4.2 Given a scenario, troubleshoot common problems related to motherboards, RAM, CPU and power with appropriate tools

28. You are troubleshooting a system that shuts down unexpectedly. What is the most likely source of the problem?

    A. A user error

    B. Overheating or faulty RAM, motherboard, or processor

    C. An application having a missing DLL file

    D. An incorrectly set property on a service

    220-802 A+ Objective 4.2 Given a scenario, troubleshoot common problems related to motherboards, RAM, CPU and power with appropriate tools appropriate tools

29. Startup BIOS communicates _____ errors as a series of beeps before it tests video.

    A. PLM

    B. CGI

    C. POST

    D. EERP

    220-802 A+ Objective 4.2 Given a scenario, troubleshoot common problems related to motherboards, RAM, CPU and power with appropriate tools appropriate tools

30. What should you do if there is smoke or a burning smell coming from a computer?

A. Immediately unplug the computer.

B. Start the computer in Safe Mode.

C. Call the manufacturer of the computer.

D. Use a power supply tester to check for correct voltage outputs.

220-802 A+ Objective 4.2 Given a scenario, troubleshoot common problems related to motherboards, RAM, CPU and power with appropriate tools appropriate tools

31. What should you do if fans spin but no power gets to other devices?

A. Immediately unplug the computer.

B. Start the computer in Safe Mode.

C. Call the manufacturer of the computer.

D. Use a power supply tester to check for correct voltage outputs.

220-802 A+ Objective 4.2 Given a scenario, troubleshoot common problems related to motherboards, RAM, CPU and power with appropriate tools

32. The easiest way to temporarily install a hard drive in a system is to use a _____ port.

A. USB

B. VGS

C. network

D. video

220-802 A+ Objective 4.2 Given a scenario, troubleshoot common problems related to motherboards, RAM, CPU and power with appropriate tools

33. If the hard drive has important data on it that has not been backed up, your first priority is most likely to _____.

A. restart the computer

B. recover the data

C. disconnect the computer from the network

D. diagnose the problem

220-802 A+ Objective 4.2 Given a scenario, troubleshoot common problems related to motherboards, RAM, CPU and power with appropriate tools

34. If the power supply is grossly inadequate, the computer's electrical system will _____ when you first plug in the power supply.

A. flare up

B. shut down

C. blink

D. whine

220-802 A+ Objective 4.2 Given a scenario, troubleshoot common problems related to motherboards, RAM, CPU and power with appropriate tools

4

35. What is most likely to happen if some component on the motherboard makes improper contact with the chassis?

   A. A software error message

   B. An application error message

   C. A short

   D. Blinking lights

   220-802 A+ Objective 4.2 Given a scenario, troubleshoot common problems related to motherboards, RAM, CPU and power with appropriate tools

36. _____ can cause intermittent errors, the system to hang, or components to fail or not last as long as they normally would.

   A. Overheating

   B. Network issues

   C. Freezing

   D. I/O issues

   220-802 A+ Objective 4.2 Given a scenario, troubleshoot common problems related to motherboards, RAM, CPU and power with appropriate tools

37. Processors can sense their operating temperatures and report that information to _____.

   A. System Restore

   B. Windows Explorer

   C. USB port

   D. BIOS

   220-802 A+ Objective 4.2 Given a scenario, troubleshoot common problems related to motherboards, RAM, CPU and power with appropriate tools

38. If the system refuses to boot or hangs after a period of activity, suspect _____.

   A. overheating

   B. power cord issues

   C. I/O issues

   D. Water damage issues

   220-802 A+ Objective 4.2 Given a scenario, troubleshoot common problems related to motherboards, RAM, CPU and power with appropriate tools

39. For better ventilation, use a power supply that has vents on the _____ of the power supply.

   A. front only

   B. left side

   C. bottom and front

   D. right side

   220-802 A+ Objective 4.2 Given a scenario, troubleshoot common problems related to motherboards, RAM, CPU and power with appropriate tools

40. Intel and AMD both recommend a(n) _____ air guide as part of the case design.

    A. open

    B. closed

    C. rack

    D. chassis

    220-802 A+ Objective 4.2 Given a scenario, troubleshoot common problems related to motherboards, RAM, CPU and power with appropriate tools

41. What is indicated by the fact that you can see error messages on a computer screen?

    A. The electrical system might not be working.

    B. Video and the electrical system are working.

    C. Memory is causing the problem.

    D. Applications are causing the problem.

    220-802 A+ Objective 4.2 Given a scenario, troubleshoot common problems related to motherboards, RAM, CPU and power with appropriate tools

42. What indicates that the computer passed all POST tests?

    A. One long and two short beeps

    B. Continuous short beeps

    C. One short beep or no beep

    D. Three long beeps

    220-802 A+ Objective 4.2 Given a scenario, troubleshoot common problems related to motherboards, RAM, CPU and power with appropriate tools

43. What beep(s) during POST indicates a motherboard problem?

    A. One long and two short beeps

    B. Continuous short beeps

    C. One short beep or no beep

    D. One long and one short beep

    220-802 A+ Objective 4.2 Given a scenario, troubleshoot common problems related to motherboards, RAM, CPU and power with appropriate tools

44. What beep(s) during POST indicates a video problem?

    A. One long and three short beeps

    B. Continuous short beeps

    C. One short beep or no beep

    D. One long and one short beep

    220-802 A+ Objective 4.2 Given a scenario, troubleshoot common problems related to motherboards, RAM, CPU and power with appropriate tools

4

45. What beep(s) during POST indicates a keyboard controller problem?

    A. One long and three short beeps

    B. Three long beeps

    C. One short beep or no beep

    D. Continuous high and low beeps

    220-802 A+ Objective 4.2 Given a scenario, troubleshoot common problems related to motherboards, RAM, CPU and power with appropriate tools

46. What beep(s) during POST indicates a CPU problem?

    A. One long and three short beeps

    B. Continuous two short beeps and then a pause

    C. One short beep or no beep

    D. Continuous high and low beeps

    220-802 A+ Objective 4.2 Given a scenario, troubleshoot common problems related to motherboards, RAM, CPU and power with appropriate tools

47. As Windows starts up, which of the following would you press to view the Advanced Boot Options menu?

    A. F1

    B. F2

    C. F5

    D. F8

    220-802 A+ Objective 4.2 Given a scenario, troubleshoot common problems related to motherboards, RAM, CPU and power with appropriate tools

48. What is a field replaceable unit (FRU) on a motherboard?

    A. Processor cooler

    B. Mouse

    C. Keyboard

    D. BIOS

    220-802 A+ Objective 4.2 Given a scenario, troubleshoot common problems related to motherboards, RAM, CPU and power with appropriate tools

49. In Windows, what is the best tool to check for potential hardware problems?

    A. Memory Diagnostics

    B. System Restore

    C. Device Manager

    D. Task Manager

    220-802 A+ Objective 4.2 Given a scenario, troubleshoot common problems related to motherboards, RAM, CPU and power with appropriate tools

50. If you cannot load the Windows desktop, press the _____ during the boot, and the Windows Boot Manager screen will appear.

    A. Spacebar

    B. Ctrl key

    C. F2

    D. F5

    220-802 A+ Objective 4.2 Given a scenario, troubleshoot common problems related to motherboards, RAM, CPU and power with appropriate tools

51. When you first install a device, Windows stores a copy of the driver software in a _____.

    A. memory bank

    B. software storage

    C. driver store

    D. driver bank

    220-802 A+ Objective 4.2 Given a scenario, troubleshoot common problems related to motherboards, RAM, CPU and power with appropriate tools

52. The Power Switch lead from the front of the case must be connected to the _____ on the motherboard.

    A. target

    B. stem

    C. header

    D. backer

    220-802 A+ Objective 4.2 Given a scenario, troubleshoot common problems related to motherboards, RAM, CPU and power with appropriate tools

53. _____ installed in case holes keep the motherboard from causing a short.

    A. Icers

    B. Spacers

    C. Boards

    D. Toners

    220-802 A+ Objective 4.2 Given a scenario, troubleshoot common problems related to motherboards, RAM, CPU and power with appropriate tools

54. Hardware problems usually show up at _____ unless there is physical damage to an area of the hard drive that is not accessed during _____.

    A. ERP

    B. Recovery

    C. POST

    D. FTP

    220-802 A+ Objective 4.3 Given a scenario, troubleshoot hard drives and RAID arrays with appropriate tools

55. For a RAID array, you can use the _____ utility to check the status of each disk in the array and to check for errors.

    A. firmware

    B. status

    C. hard drive

    D. IDE

    220-802 A+ Objective 4.3 Given a scenario, troubleshoot hard drives and RAID arrays with appropriate tools

56. Regardless of how an external enclosure connects to a computer or network, the hard drives inside the enclosure might use a SATA or _____ connection.

    A. USB

    B. PATA

    C. FTP

    D. BIOS

    220-802 A+ Objective 4.3 Given a scenario, troubleshoot hard drives and RAID arrays with appropriate tools

57. A _____ motherboard used with an Energy Saver monitor can be configured to go into standby or sleep mode after a period of inactivity.

    A. Compact

    B. Circular

    C. Saver

    D. Green

    220-802 A+ Objective 4.4 Given a scenario, troubleshoot common video and display issues

58. What term refers to pixels on an LCD monitor that are not working?

    A. Stones

    B. Dead pixels

    C. Broken pixels

    D. Pot holes

    220-802 A+ Objective 4.4 Given a scenario, troubleshoot common video and display issues

59. A(n) _____ pixel is likely to be a broken transistor that cannot be fixed.

    A. green

    B. orange or red

    C. black or white

    D. blue

    220-802 A+ Objective 4.4 Given a scenario, troubleshoot common video and display issues

60. Horizontally torn images on-screen are called _____.
    A. stones
    B. artifacts
    C. dead displays
    D. frozen pixels
    220-802 A+ Objective 4.4 Given a scenario, troubleshoot common video and display issues

61. What is most likely to cause monitor flicker?
    A. Overclocking
    B. BIOS
    C. Firmware
    D. Poor cable connections
    220-802 A+ Objective 4.4 Given a scenario, troubleshoot common video and display

62. Odd-colored blotches on the screen or a screen flicker might indicate that a device such as a speaker or fan is sitting too close to the monitor and emitting electrical noise called _____.
    A. FTP
    B. SFP
    C. EMI
    D. RFID
    220-802 A+ Objective 4.4 Given a scenario, troubleshoot common video and display issues

63. Some monitors have a _____ button to eliminate accumulated or stray magnetic fields.
    A. degauss
    B. target
    C. de-magnetize
    D. rotate
    220-802 A+ Objective 4.4 Given a scenario, troubleshoot common video and display issues

64. When the display settings do not work, you can easily return to standard _____ settings called _____ mode.
    A. BTS
    B. STP
    C. IMMP
    D. VGA
    220-802 A+ Objective 4.4 Given a scenario, troubleshoot common video and display issues

4

65. A POST diagnostic card is also called a(n) _____ test card.

    A. electricity

    B. motherboard

    C. hard drive

    D. bay

    220-802 A+ Objective 4.2 Given a scenario, troubleshoot common problems related to motherboards, RAM, CPU and power with appropriate tools

66. A(n) _____ can be of great help to discover and report computer errors and conflicts that occur when you first turn on a computer and before the operating system is launched.

    A. network cable tester

    B. electric tester

    C. I/O card

    D. POST card

    220-802 A+ Objective 4.2 Given a scenario, troubleshoot common problems related to motherboards, RAM, CPU and power with appropriate tools

67. BIOS is an acronym for _____.

    A. base input/output standard

    B. broad input/output standard

    C. basic input/output system

    D. broad input/output system

    220-802 A+ Objective 4.2 Given a scenario, troubleshoot common problems related to motherboards, RAM, CPU and power with appropriate tools

68. The BIOS programs are stored on a special _____ chip.

    A. RAM

    B. ROM

    C. FTP

    D. STTP

    220-802 A+ Objective 4.2 Given a scenario, troubleshoot common problems related to motherboards, RAM, CPU and power with appropriate tools

69. What is another term for BIOS programs?

    A. Firmware

    B. Battery chip

    C. Start programs

    D. System programs

    220-802 A+ Objective 4.2 Given a scenario, troubleshoot common problems related to motherboards, RAM, CPU and power with appropriate tools

70. _____ manages essential devices (such as the keyboard, mouse, hard drive, and monitor) before the OS is launched.

A. Startup BIOS

B. BIOS setup

C. CMOS setup

D. System BIOS

220-802 A+ Objective 4.2 Given a scenario, troubleshoot common problems related to motherboards, RAM, CPU and power with appropriate tools

71. _____ is used to start the computer.

A. Startup BIOS

B. BIOS setup

C. CMOS setup

D. System BIOS

220-802 A+ Objective 4.2 Given a scenario, troubleshoot common problems related to motherboards, RAM, CPU and power with appropriate tools

72. _____ is used to change the motherboard configuration or settings.

A. Startup BIOS

B. PCI setup

C. CMOS setup

D. System BIOS

220-802 A+ Objective 4.2 Given a scenario, troubleshoot common problems related to motherboards, RAM, CPU and power with appropriate tools

73. What refers to a series of tests performed by the startup BIOS when you first turn on a computer?

A. ERT

B. CMD

C. STP

D. POST

220-802 A+ Objective 4.2 Given a scenario, troubleshoot common problems related to motherboards, RAM, CPU and power with appropriate tools

74. A power supply tester is used to measure the output of each _____ coming from the power supply.

A. spacer

B. connector

C. tablet

D. staple

220-802 A+ Objective 4.2 Given a scenario, troubleshoot common problems related to motherboards, RAM, CPU and power with appropriate tools

4

75. A(n) _____ is a general-purpose tool that can measure several characteristics of electricity in a variety of devices.

   A. conductor

   B. electric tester

   C. multimeter

   D. device meter

   220-802 A+ Objective 4.2 Given a scenario, troubleshoot common problems related to motherboards, RAM, CPU and power with appropriate tools

76. What determines that two ends of a cable or fuse are connected without interruption?

   A. Continuity

   B. Loopback

   C. Resistance

   D. Voltage

   220-802 A+ Objective 4.2 Given a scenario, troubleshoot common problems related to motherboards, RAM, CPU and power with appropriate tools

77. What is used to test a port in a computer or other device to make sure the port is working?

   A. Continuity tester

   B. Loopback plug

   C. Multimeter

   D. Voltage conductor

   220-802 A+ Objective 4.2 Given a scenario, troubleshoot common problems related to motherboards, RAM, CPU and power with appropriate tools

78. What is the best tool to test the throughput or speed of a port?

   A. Multimeter

   B. Voltage conductor

   C. Continuity tester

   D. Loopback plug

   220-802 A+ Objective 4.2 Given a scenario, troubleshoot common problems related to motherboards, RAM, CPU and power with appropriate tools

79. What term refers to the computer bringing itself up to a working state without the user having to do anything but press the on button?

   A. Skating

   B. Churning

   C. Booting

   D. Loading

   220-802 A+ Objective 4.6 Given a scenario, troubleshoot operating system problems with appropriate tools

80. A hard boot is also referred to as a(n) _____ boot.

   A. cold

   B. warm

   C. circular

   D. intermediate

   220-802 A+ Objective 4.6 Given a scenario, troubleshoot operating system problems with appropriate tools

81. A(n) _____ boot involves turning on the power with the on/off switch.

   A. intermediate

   B. soft

   C. circular

   D. cold

   220-802 A+ Objective 4.6 Given a scenario, troubleshoot operating system problems with appropriate tools

82. What is another term for a warm boot?

   A. Intermediate boot

   B. Soft boot

   C. Circular boot

   D. Cold boot

   220-802 A+ Objective 4.6 Given a scenario, troubleshoot operating system problems with appropriate tools

83. What is true about a hard boot?

   A. It initializes the processor and clears memory.

   B. It takes less time than a soft boot.

   C. It has fewer steps than a soft boot.

   D. It is performed using the operating system.

   220-802 A+ Objective 4.6 Given a scenario, troubleshoot operating system problems with appropriate tools

84. A successful boot depends on the hardware, the BIOS, and the _____ all performing without errors.

   A. applications

   B. network

   C. operating system

   D. I/O

   220-802 A+ Objective 4.6 Given a scenario, troubleshoot operating system problems with appropriate tools

4

85. Future desktop and notebook systems are likely to use replacement technologies for the BIOS firmware on the motherboard. What is one newer standard for the interface between the firmware on the motherboard and the operating system?

    A. BCD

    B. EFI

    C. ERP

    D. MRB

    220-802 A+ Objective 4.6 Given a scenario, troubleshoot operating system problems with appropriate tools

86. What contains the partition table and the master boot program that is used to locate and start the BootMgr program?

    A. MBR

    B. Hal.dll

    C. OS boot record

    D. BCD

    220-802 A+ Objective 4.6 Given a scenario, troubleshoot operating system problems with appropriate tools

87. The Boot Configuration Data file is organized in the same manner as a _____.

    A. network drive

    B. node

    C. circular bay

    D. registry hive

    220-802 A+ Objective 4.6 Given a scenario, troubleshoot operating system problems with appropriate tools

88. The MBR program searches the partition table for the _____ partition, which Windows calls the system partition.

    A. active

    B. inactive

    C. sectional

    D. startup

    220-802 A+ Objective 4.6 Given a scenario, troubleshoot operating system problems with appropriate tools

89. When starting XP, the MBR looks for the first sector in the active partition, which is called the _____ record.

    A. churn

    B. memory

    C. OS boot

    D. network

    220-802 A+ Objective 4.6 Given a scenario, troubleshoot operating system problems with appropriate tools

90. _____ reads XP settings used for the boot stored in Boot.ini.

    A. Ntldr

    B. BCD

    C. Mgr

    D. Ltr

    220-802 A+ Objective 4.6 Given a scenario, troubleshoot operating system problems with appropriate tools

91. _____ Mode boots the OS with a minimum configuration and can be used to solve problems with a new hardware installation, a corrupted Windows installation, or problems caused by user settings.

    A. Secure

    B. Basic

    C. Safe

    D. Default

    220-802 A+ Objective 4.6 Given a scenario, troubleshoot operating system problems with appropriate tools

92. Use _____ to disable unneeded services or startup processes.

    A. Diagnostics

    B. Event Viewer

    C. Process Services

    D. System Configuration

    220-802 A+ Objective 4.6 Given a scenario, troubleshoot operating system problems with appropriate tools

93. What command can be used to check for file system errors?

    A. sfc /scannow

    B. chkdsk /r

    C. ntbtlog.txt

    D. sys/check

    220-802 A+ Objective 4.6 Given a scenario, troubleshoot operating system problems with appropriate tools

94 _____ is a lean operating system that can be launched to solve Windows startup problems after other tools available on the Advanced Boot Options menu have failed to solve the problem.

    A. Windows DR

    B. Windows LTE

    C. Windows RE

    D. Windows IDE

    220-802 A+ Objective 4.6 Given a scenario, troubleshoot operating system problems with appropriate tools

4

95. One possible method when attempting to repair a corrupted file system is to use the command prompt window and the _____ command.

   A. chkdsk c: /r

   B. chk file

   C. disc c: /f

   D. disc scan

   220-802 A+ Objective 4.3 Given a scenario, troubleshoot hard drives and RAID arrays with appropriate tools

96. To recover data from a computer that will not boot, one technique is to use a SATA-to-_____ converter to recover data from a drive using a SATA connector.

   A. BOIS

   B. NTS

   C. USB

   D. FTP

   220-802 A+ Objective 4.3 Given a scenario, troubleshoot hard drives and RAID arrays with appropriate tools

97. A _____ can be used to test a cable to find out if it is good or to determine the type of cable if it is not labeled.

   A. cable tester

   B. cable checker

   C. cable rod

   D. cable tip

   220-802 A+ Objective 4.5 Given a scenario, troubleshoot wired and wireless networks with appropriate tools

98. What can be used to trace a network cable through a building?

   A. cable tester

   B. cable checker

   C. cable rod

   D. cable tip

   220-802 A+ Objective 4.5 Given a scenario, troubleshoot wired and wireless networks with appropriate tools

99. A loopback plug can be used to test _____.

   A. whether a remote computer is online

   B. a cable that is not live

   C. a live network cable

   D. the strength of an RF signal

   220-802 A+ Objective 4.5 Given a scenario, troubleshoot wired and wireless networks with appropriate tools

100. A wireless locator helps you find a(n) _____ hotspot.

    A. Ethernet

    B. Wi-Fi

    C. CSS

    D. TCP

    220-802 A+ Objective 4.5 Given a scenario, troubleshoot wired and wireless networks with appropriate tools

101. The _____ command tests connectivity by sending an echo request to a remote computer.

    A. test

    B. net

    C. ping

    D. ipconfig

    220-802 A+ Objective 4.5 Given a scenario, troubleshoot wired and wireless networks with appropriate tools

102. The _____ command can display TCP/IP configuration information and refresh the TCP/IP assignments to a connection including its IP address.

    A. ping

    B. net

    C. cssd

    D. ipconfig

    220-802 A+ Objective 4.5 Given a scenario, troubleshoot wired and wireless networks with appropriate tools

103. What command leases a new IP address from a DHCP server?

    A. ipconfig /renew

    B. ipconfig /release

    C. ipconfig /all

    D. ipconfig /flushdns

    220-802 A+ Objective 4.5 Given a scenario, troubleshoot wired and wireless networks with appropriate tools

104. What command displays TCP/IP information?

    A. ipconfig /renew

    B. ipconfig /release

    C. ipconfig /all

    D. ipconfig /flushdns

    220-802 A+ Objective 4.5 Given a scenario, troubleshoot wired and wireless networks with appropriate tools

4

105. _____ lets you read information from the Internet name space by requesting information about domain name resolutions from the DNS server's zone data.

A. Ipconfig

B. Nslookup

C. Ping

D. Net

220-802 A+ Objective 4.5 Given a scenario, troubleshoot wired and wireless networks with appropriate tools

106. _____ messages are used by routers and hosts to communicate error messages and updates.

A. TCP

B. IP

C. REST

D. ICMP

220-802 A+ Objective 4.5 Given a scenario, troubleshoot wired and wireless networks with appropriate tools

107. To check for local connectivity, use _____ to try to access shared folders on the network.

A. Task Manager

B. Disk Explorer

C. Windows Explorer

D. Memory Diagnostics

220-802 A+ Objective 4.5 Given a scenario, troubleshoot wired and wireless networks with appropriate tools

108. To find out if a computer with limited or no connectivity was able to initially connect to a DHCP server on the network, check for a(n) _____.

A. APIPA

B. IP address

C. network ID

D. CCDIA

220-802 A+ Objective 4.5 Given a scenario, troubleshoot wired and wireless networks with appropriate tools

109. A computer assigns itself an APIPA if it is unable to find a DHCP server when it first attempts to connect to a network. What command can be used to determine the IP address?

A. nslookup

B. ping

C. net

D. ipconfig

220-802 A+ Objective 4.5 Given a scenario, troubleshoot wired and wireless networks with appropriate tools

110. If the router or switch is in a server closet and the ports are not well labeled, you can use a _____ to find out which port the computer is using.

   A. network tracer

   B. loopback plug

   C. network router

   D. port plug

   220-802 A+ Objective 4.5 Given a scenario, troubleshoot wired and wireless networks with appropriate tools

111. A _____ can be attached on a network cable near a phone port to help to eliminate electromagnetic interference (EMI).

   A. ferrite clamp

   B. loopback plug

   C. port plug

   D. de-magnetizer

   220-802 A+ Objective 4.5 Given a scenario, troubleshoot wired and wireless networks with appropriate tools

112. If you are having a problem accessing a particular computer on the Internet, try using the _____ command. The results show computers along the route that might be giving delays.

   A. ipconfig

   B. network trace

   C. tracert

   D. track

   220-802 A+ Objective 4.5 Given a scenario, troubleshoot wired and wireless networks with appropriate tools

113. To see the priority order and determine which connection is faster, use the Networking tab of _____.

   A. Device Manager

   B. Windows Explorer

   C. Start menu

   D. Task Manager

   220-802 A+ Objective 4.5 Given a scenario, troubleshoot wired and wireless networks with appropriate tools

4

114. If you encounter a problem when installing Windows 7 using RAID or SCSI drives (such as an undetected RAID or SCSI hard drive), know that the problem is a(n) _____ or firmware problem and not a Windows setup problem.

    A. hardware

    B. software

    C. application

    D. network

    220-802 A+ Objective 4.6 Given a scenario, troubleshoot operating system problems with appropriate tools

115. If the system is experiencing a marked decrease in performance, suspect a(n) _____.

    A. electric problem

    B. network issue

    C. virus

    D. BIOS issue

    220-802 A+ Objective 4.3 Given a scenario, troubleshoot hard drives and RAID arrays with appropriate tools

116. To ensure better performance in a Windows system, make sure at least _____ percent of drive C: is free.

    A. 10

    B. 15

    C. 20

    D. 30

    220-802 A+ Objective 4.3 Given a scenario, troubleshoot hard drives and RAID arrays with appropriate tools

117. If a performance problem exists in Safe Mode, you can assume that the problem is with the _____ or with Windows settings.

    A. network

    B. browser

    C. hardware

    D. operating system

    220-802 A+ Objective 4.3 Given a scenario, troubleshoot hard drives and RAID arrays with appropriate tools

118. What is a tool used to monitor the startup process?

    A. WinPatrol

    B. WinStart

    C. StartMonitor

    D. IPTrack

    220-802 A+ Objective 4.3 Given a scenario, troubleshoot hard drives and RAID arrays with appropriate tools

119. Many _____ monitor the startup process and inform you when changes are made.

A. productivity tools

B. browsers

C. hardware programs

D. antivirus programs

220-802 A+ Objective 4.3 Given a scenario, troubleshoot hard drives and RAID arrays with appropriate tools

120. Use the _____ to locate information about the installed processor and its speed, how much RAM is installed, and the amount of free space on the hard drive.

A. Task Manager

B. Device Manager

C. System Information Utility

D. System Verification Tool

220-802 A+ Objective 4.3 Given a scenario, troubleshoot hard drives and RAID arrays with appropriate tools

121. The Windows 7/Vista _____ is responsible for maintaining an index of files and folders on a hard drive to speed up Windows searches.

A. tracker

B. indexer

C. version control

D. mapper

220-802 A+ Objective 4.3 Given a scenario, troubleshoot hard drives and RAID arrays with appropriate tools

122. If you notice that performance slows after a system has been up and running without a restart for some time, suspect a _____.

A. memory leak

B. network problem

C. BIOS problem

D. startup failure

220-802 A+ Objective 4.3 Given a scenario, troubleshoot hard drives and RAID arrays with appropriate tools

123. A _____ is caused when an application does not properly release allocated memory that it no longer needs and continually requests more memory than it needs.

A. startup failure

B. memory leak

C. memory gap

D. BIOS fail

220-802 A+ Objective 4.3 Given a scenario, troubleshoot hard drives and RAID arrays with appropriate tools

4

124. You can manually have Windows test a memory card or flash drive for _____ by right-clicking the device and selecting Properties from the shortcut menu.

    A. ReadyBoost

    B. FlashBoost

    C. Flash Performance

    D. SD Advantage

    220-802 A+ Objective 4.3 Given a scenario, troubleshoot hard drives and RAID arrays with appropriate tools

125. The Windows _____ interface might slow down a system because it uses memory and computing power.

    A. Xeon

    B. Panther

    C. Aero

    D. Tracker

    220-802 A+ Objective 4.3 Given a scenario, troubleshoot hard drives and RAID arrays with appropriate tools

126. The Vista sidebar appears on the Windows desktop to hold apps called _____.

    A. tools

    B. utilities

    C. units

    D. gadgets

    220-802 A+ Objective 4.3 Given a scenario, troubleshoot hard drives and RAID arrays with appropriate tools

127. Most programs written for Windows have an uninstall routine that can be accessed from the Windows 7/Vista Programs and Features window, the XP Add Remove Programs window, or an uninstall utility in the _____ menu.

    A. Properties

    B. All Programs

    C. Options

    D. Designer

    220-802 A+ Objective 4.3 Given a scenario, troubleshoot hard drives and RAID arrays with appropriate tools

128. It is wise to back up the registry before opening the Registry Editor using the
     _____ command in the search box.

     A. regedit

     B. registry

     C. open reg

     D. track reg

     220-802 A+ Objective 4.3 Given a scenario, troubleshoot hard drives and RAID arrays with
     appropriate tools

129. To remove a program from the All Programs menu, right-click it and select
     _____ from the shortcut menu.

     A. Remove

     B. Options

     C. Delete

     D. Uninstall

     220-802 A+ Objective 4.3 Given a scenario, troubleshoot hard drives and RAID arrays with
     appropriate tools

130. After manually deleting a program, if you see an error about a missing program file, use
     _____ to find out how the program is set to start.

     A. ipconfig

     B. ping

     C. start trace

     D. msconfig

     220-802 A+ Objective 4.3 Given a scenario, troubleshoot hard drives and RAID arrays with
     appropriate tools

4

Part III

CompTIA A+ Exam Answers

CompTIA A+ Exam 220-801 Answers

CompTIA A+ Exam 220-802 Answers

1.0–5.0

COMPTIA A+
EXAM 220-801 ANSWERS

DOMAIN 1.0 PC HARDWARE

Question	Answer	Explanation
1	C	To find the correct user guide online, you need to know the board manufacturer and model.
2	A	A program in BIOS, called BIOS setup or CMOS setup, can easily make changes to the setup values stored in CMOS RAM.
3	C	Unified Extensible Firmware Interface (UEFI) is an interface between firmware on the motherboard and the operating system and improves on processes for booting, handing over the boot to the OS, and loading device drivers and applications before the OS loads.
4	C	After the OS is installed, to prevent accidental boots from a DVD or other media, change setup BIOS to boot first from the hard drive.
5	D	A jumper is two small posts or metal pins that stick up off the motherboard that is open or closed. An open jumper has no cover, and a closed jumper has a cover on the two pins.
6	C	Jumpers can be set to clear both passwords.
7	C	The process of upgrading or refreshing the programming stored on the firmware chip is called updating the BIOS or flashing BIOS.
8	B	Update your BIOS only if you're having a problem with your motherboard or there's a new BIOS feature you want to use.
9	A	You access the BIOS setup program by pressing a key or combination of keys during the boot process.
10	D	Ports coming directly off the motherboard are called on-board ports or integrated components.
11	B	The most popular motherboard form factors are ATX, microATX (a smaller version of ATX), and Mini-ITX (a smaller version of microATX).

A

Question	Answer	Explanation
12	B	MicroATX reduces the total cost of a system by reducing the number of expansion slots on the motherboard, reducing the power supplied to the board, and allowing for a smaller case size.
13	D	The computer case, sometimes called the chassis, houses the power supply, motherboard, processor, memory modules, expansion cards, hard drive, optical drive, and other drives.
14	A	The LGA2011 is used in high-end gaming and server computers and might require a liquid cooling system.
15	C	The LGA1155 is currently the most popular Intel socket.
16	B	A bus that does not run in sync with the system clock is called an expansion bus.
17	A	Most buses today are local buses, meaning that they run in sync with the system clock.
18	A	The first PCI bus had a 32-bit data path, supplied 5 V of power to an adapter card, and operated at 33 MHz.
19	C	Throughput is sometimes called bandwidth.
20	D	PCI-X focused on the server market; therefore, it's unlikely you'll see PCI-X slots in desktop computers.
21	C	PCI Express uses a serial bus, which is faster than a parallel bus because it transmits data in packets similar to how an Ethernet network, USB, and FireWire transmit data.
22	D	To reduce the amount of electrical "noise," or interference, on a SCSI cable, each end of the SCSI chain has a terminating resistor.
23	B	DMA transfers data directly from the drive to memory without involving the CPU.
24	B	A motherboard might have several internal connectors, including parallel ATA (PATA) connectors (also called IDE connectors), a floppy drive connector, serial ATA (SATA) connectors, SCSI connectors, a USB connector, or a FireWire (IEEE 1394) connector.
25	D	The riser card installs in the slot and provides another slot at a right angle.
26	B	Two standards that hard drives, optical drives, and tape drives use for both types of connections are the faster serial ATA (SATA) standard and the slower and older parallel ATA (PATA) standard.
27	C	An expansion card, also called an adapter card, is a circuit board that provides more ports than those provided by the motherboard.

Question	Answer	Explanation
28	B	A motherboard has memory slots, called DIMM (dual inline memory module) slots, to hold memory modules.
29	A	A hard drive, also called a hard disk drive (HDD), is permanent storage used to hold data and programs.
30	D	The 24-pin P1 connector, also called the 20+4 pin connector, is the main motherboard power connector used today.
31	C	A DVI (Digital Video Interface) port transmits digital or analog video.
32	D	A FireWire port (also called an IEEE1394 port, pronounced "I-triple-E 1394 port") is used for high-speed multimedia devices such as digital camcorders.
33	A	A DisplayPort transmits digital video and audio (not analog transmissions) and is slowly replacing VGA and DVI ports on personal computers.
34	C	A power supply that provides this 4-pin 12 volt power cord is called an ATX12V power supply.
35	D	A 4-pin Molex connector is used for IDE (PATA) drives.
36	B	The 8-pin PCIe connector provides an extra +12 V for high-end video cards using PCI Express, Version 2.
37	C	Wires leading from the front of the computer case to the motherboardare called the front panel connectors.
38	B	*Reset SW* is the switch used to reboot the computer.
39	C	*HDD LED* controls the drive activity light on the front panel that lights up when any SATA or IDE device is in use.
40	B	The two major manufacturers of processors are Intel and AMD.
41	C	Multiple processors can be installed in the same processor housing (called multi-core processing).
42	A	Memory on the processor die is called Level 1 cache (L1 cache).
43	D	SRAM is faster than DRAM because it does not need refreshing; it can hold its data as long as power is available.
44	B	Most processors sold today support virtualization; the feature must be enabled in BIOS setup.
45	D	A hybrid processor can use a 32-bit operating system or a 64-bit OS.
46	B	To handle two threads, the processor requires extra registers, or holding areas, within the processor housing that it uses to switch between threads. In effect, you have two logical processors for each physical processor or core. Intel calls this technology Hyper-Threading and AMD calls it HyperTransport.

A

Question	Answer	Explanation
47	A	The GPU might be on a video card on the motherboard, or embedded in the CPU package. When inside the CPU package, it is called integrated graphics.
48	C	You can view the actual processor frequency and the clock speed using the BIOS setup screens.
49	D	The cooler sits on top of the processor and consists of a fan and a heat sink.
50	B	The thermal compound transmits heat better than air and makes an airtight connection between the fan and the processor.
51	B	A 4-pin header on the motherboard supports pulse width modulation (PWM) that controls fan speed in order to reduce the overall noise in a system.
52	A	With liquid cooling, a small pump sits inside the computer case, and tubes move liquid around components and then away from them to a place where fans can cool the liquid.
53	C	The form factor of a power supply determines the size of the power supply and the placement of screw holes and slots used to anchor the power supply to the case.
54	C	A rail is the term used to describe each voltage line of the power supply. The +12 V rail is the most used, especially in high-end gaming systems.
55	D	To know what size power supply you need, add up the wattage requirements of all components, and add 30 percent.
56	A	Video cards draw the most power in a system, and they draw from the +12 V output.
57	D	If you ever need to change the dual-voltage selector switch, first turn off the computer and unplug the power supply.
58	B	Virtualization is when one physical machine hosts multiple activities that are normally done on multiple machines.
59	C	The requirements for a desktop computer that will be used to run multiple virtual machines are as follows: • Each VM has its own virtual processor, so the processor should be a multicore processor. • You need extra amounts of RAM when a computer is running several VMs. • Each VM must have an operating system installed, with adequate hard drive space for each VM.

Question	Answer	Explanation
60	D	Gaming PCs built by iBUYPOWER: Several of the PCs use liquid cooling, and all use a powerful processor with at least 8 GB of RAM.
61	C	A custom-built HTPC should include these features: • Applications software. The application controls the user interface and plays and records music and video. • HDMI port to connect video output to television. Be sure to use a high-quality HDMI cable. • Cable TV input. The best solution is to use a TV tuner card to connect the TV coax cable directly to the computer.
62	B	One popular type of home server PC is Slingbox by Sling Media.
63	A	A person who uses graphics or CAD/CAM (computer-aided design/computer-aided manufacturing) workstations might include an engineer working with CAD software to design bridges, an architect who designs skyscrapers, a graphics designer who creates artistic pages for children's books, or a landscape designer who creates lawn and garden plans.
64	B	To provide the best 3D graphics experience, use a high-end video card. The Quadro family of graphics processors has the best performing GPUs on the market, and the Quadro 6000 is the best Quadro currently sold.
65	D	Most users will require dual or triple monitors. You might need to consider dual video cards for optimum video performance or for more than two video ports.
66	C	Windows 7 can be used as the OS, but Windows Home Server 2011 provides the additional security features needed to better secure a home network. In addition, if the customer plans to use the PC to back up files on client computers, know that Windows Home Server provides a more robust backup utility than does Windows 7.

A

Question	Answer	Explanation
67	A	Features and hardware you need to consider when customizing a home server PC include: • Use a processor with moderate power. The Intel Core i5 or Core i3 works well. A moderate amount of RAM is sufficient, for example, 6 to 8 GB. • Storage speed and capacity need to be maximized. Use hardware RAID implemented on the motherboard to provide fault tolerance and high performance. Make sure the motherboard supports hardware RAID. Use fast hard drives (at least 7200 RPM) with plenty of storage capacity. Make sure the case has plenty of room for all the hard drives a customer might require. • Network transfers need to be fast, especially for streaming videos and movies. Make sure the network port is rated for Gigabit Ethernet (1000 Mbps). All other devices and computers on the LAN should also use Gigabit Ethernet. • Printer sharing. A USB printer can be connected directly to the PC and then you can use Windows to share the printer with others on the network. Alternately, some routers and switches provide a USB port that can be used to connect a USB printer to other computers on the network. • Onboard video works well. Recall that onboard video is a video port embedded on the motherboard and does not perform as well as a good video card. Because the PC is not likely to be used as a workstation, you don't need powerful video.
68	C	A zero client, also called a dumb terminal, is built by the manufacturer. It does not have an OS and is little more than an interface to the network with a keyboard, monitor, and mouse.
69	A	A thin client is a computer that has an operating system but has little computer power and might only need to support a browser used to communicate with the server.
70	C	A thick client, also called a fat client, is a regular desktop computer or laptop that is sometimes used as a client by a virtualization server.
71	D	When using the LGA2011 socket, liquid cooling is a Microsoft recommendation.
72	B	DRAM loses its data rapidly, and the memory controller must refresh it several thousand times a second.
73	C	Random access memory (RAM) temporarily holds data and instructions as the CPU processes them. RAM is stored on memory modules, which are installed in memory slots on the motherboard.

Question	Answer	Explanation
74	A	All new motherboards for desktops sold today use a type of memory module called a DIMM (dual inline memory module).
75	C	Laptops use a smaller version of a DIMM called a SO-DIMM (small outline DIMM and pronounced "sew-dim").
76	D	240-pin DDR3 DIMM is currently the fastest memory. It can support quad, triple, or dual channels or be installed as a single DIMM.
77	C	240-pin DDR2 DIMM can support dual channels or be installed as a single DIMM. It has one notch near the center of the edge connector.
78	B	184-pin DDR DIMM can support dual channels or be installed as a single DIMM. It has one offset notch.
79	A	The first DIMM to run synchronized with the system clock was synchronous DRAM (SDRAM), which has two notches and uses 168 pins.
80	D	RIMM has 184 pins and two notches near the center of the edge connector.
81	C	Even though an older RAM technology is no longer used by new motherboards, RAM manufacturers continue to produce the older RAM because older motherboards require these replacement modules. SIMMs and RIMMs are now obsolete.
82	B	A PCI Express ×1 slot contains a single lane for data; this lane is actually four wires.
83	A	DDR runs twice as fast as regular SDRAM, has one notch, and uses 184 pins. Instead of processing data for each beat of the system clock, as with regular SDRAM, it processes data when the beat rises and again when it falls, doubling the data rate of memory.
84	B	Sandy Bridge technology introduced quad channels, where the processor can access four DIMMs at the same time.
85	C	For dual, triple, or quad channels to work, the motherboard and the DIMM must support the technology.
86	B	When setting up dual channeling, the pair of DIMMs in a channel must be equally matched in size, speed, and features, and it is recommended they come from the same manufacturer.
87	B	To get the highest performance, memory slots are placed on either side of the processor in order to shorten the length of the memory bus.
88	A	A PC rating is a measure of the total bandwidth of data moving between the module and the CPU.
89	B	A network printer is identified on the network by its IP address
90	D	A DIMM can have memory chips installed on one side of the module (called single-sided) or both sides of the module (called double-sided).

A

Question	Answer	Explanation
91	C	ECC memory costs more than non-ECC memory, but it is more reliable.
92	D	Later, when the byte is read back, the memory controller checks the odd or even state.
93	A	With RIMMs, each memory slot on the motherboard must be filled to maintain continuity throughout all slots.
94	B	If you install modules of different speeds in the same system, the system will run at the slowest speed or might become unstable.
95	C	BIOS setup reports the memory configuration and amount.
96	B	The limit for a 32-bit OS is 4 GB installed RAM.
97	D	To help with airflow, try to leave an empty slot between cards. In particular, try to leave an empty slot beside the video card, which puts off a lot of heat.
98	C	Error messages about video appear when Windows starts. This can be caused by a conflict in onboard video and the video card. Try disabling onboard video in Device Manager.
99	A	A sound card (an expansion card with sound ports) or onboard sound (sound ports embedded on a motherboard) can play and record sound, and then save it in a file.
100	C	A sound card (an expansion card with sound ports) or onboard sound (sound ports embedded on a motherboard) can play and record sound, and save it in a file.
101	B	A TV tuner card can turn your computer into a television. A port on the card receives input from a TV cable and lets you view television on your computer monitor.
102	A	A video capture card lets you capture video input and save it to a file on your hard drive.
103	B	When installing a TV tuner or capture card, you will most likely install the drivers, install the card, and then install the application software that comes bundled with the card. You can then configure and manage the card using the applications.
104	C	The CRT (cathode-ray tube) monitor was first used in television sets, takes up a lot of desk space, and is now largely obsolete.
105	A	The LCD (liquid crystal display) monitor, also called a flat-panel monitor, was first used in laptops.
106	D	A plasma monitor provides high contrast with better color than LCD monitors.

Question	Answer	Explanation
107	B	Backlighting is used to light the LCD panel. The trend for most monitor manufacturers is to use LED backlighting, which provides a better range and accuracy of color and uses less power than earlier technologies.
108	A	An OLED (Organic Light-emitting Diode) monitor uses a thin LED layer or film between two grids of electrodes. OLED screens provide better contrast, work in darker rooms, and use less power than an LCD monitor.
109	C	The refresh rate, also called the response time, is the time it takes for a monitor to build one screen, measured in ms (milliseconds) or Hz (hertz).
110	B	The resolution is the number of spots or pixels on a screen that can be addressed by software.
111	D	The native resolution is the number of pixels built into the LCD monitor.
112	B	Brightness is measured in cd/m2 (candela per square meter), which is the same as lumens/m2 (lumens per square meter).
113	C	A video card can use an AGP, PCI, or PCI Express slot on the motherboard. The fastest slot to use is a PCIe x16 slot.
114	D	The 15-pin VGA port is the standard analog video port and transmits three signals of red, green, and blue (RGB).
115	B	The DVI-I port supports both analog and digital signals.
116	C	Composite video does not produce as sharp an image as VGA video or S-Video.
117	A	The HDMI standards allow for several types of HDMI connectors. The best known, which is used on most computers and televisions, is the Type A 19-pin HDMI connector.
118	D	A few older video cameras use a 6-pin variation of S-Video. The connector is called a MiniDin-6 connector and looks like a PS/2 connector used by a keyboard or mouse.
119	A	10Base2 (ThinNet) 10 Mbps: Coaxial cable uses a BNC connector.
120	C	100BaseT (Fast Ethernet): Twisted pair (UTP or STP) uses an RJ-45 connector.
121	B	The two most popular internal drive interfaces are Parallel ATA (PATA) and Serial ATA (SATA).
122	D	SATA III or SATA3: 6 Gb/sec
123	C	Solid state drives are much more expensive than magnetic hard drives, but they are faster, more reliable, last longer, and use less power than magnetic drives.
124	B	The spindle rotates at 5400, 7200, 10,000, or 15,000 RPM (revolutions per minute).

A

Question	Answer	Explanation
125	A	SD cards come in three physical sizes: Full-size SD, MiniSD, and MicroSD.
126	D	The xD-Picture Card has a compact design (about the size of a postage stamp), and currently holds up to 8 GB of data.
127	A	RAID 0 also uses two or more physical disks to increase the disk space available for a single volume. RAID 0 writes to the physical disks evenly across all disks so that no one disk receives all the activity, and therefore improves performance.
128	C	RAID 5 stripes data across three or more drives and uses parity checking, so that if one drive fails, the other drives can re-create the data stored on the failed drive by using the parity information.
129	B	It takes at least four disks for RAID 10. Data is mirrored across pairs of disks.
130	C	An internal tape drive can interface with a computer using a SCSI, PATA, or SATA connection.
131	D	When connecting the data cable, align the edge color of the ribbon cable with pin 1 on the motherboard connector.
132	B	Device manufacturers often release updates to device drivers. Update the drivers to solve problems with the device or to add new features. You can use Device Manager in Windows to manage devices and their drivers.
133	C	A TV tuner card in a PCI slot will not work as fast as a TV tuner card in a PCI Express slot because of the different speeds of the slots.
134	C	Wi-Fi 802.11n (RF of 2.4 GHz or 5.0 GHz): Up to 500 Mbps Wi-Fi 802.11g (RF of 2.4 GHz): Up to 54 Mbps Wi-Fi 802.11b (RF of 2.4 GHz): Up to 11 Mbps
135	A	FireWire 800 (also called 1394b): Cable lengths up to 100 meters
136	D	This USB 3.0 B-Male connector is used by SuperSpeed USB 3.0 devices such as printers or scanners.
137	A	A network port, also called an Ethernet port, or an RJ-45 port, is used by a network cable to connect to the wired network.
138	D	Analog means a continuous signal with infinite variations.
139	B	On a PC, the purple port is for the keyboard, and the green port is for the mouse.
140	C	All PATA standards since ATA-2 support this configuration of four IDE devices in a system, which is called the Enhanced IDE (EIDE) standard.
141	B	An optical drive must follow the ATAPI (Advanced Technology Attachment Packet Interface) standard in order to connect to a system using an IDE connector.

Question	Answer	Explanation
142	A	A parallel port is a 25-pin female port used by older printers.
143	D	All the devices and the host adapter form a single daisy chain.
144	B	The most popular SCSI connectors are 50-pin, A-cable connectors for narrow SCSI, and 68-pin, P-cable connectors for wide SCSI.
145	A	For external drives, common standards are eSATA, FireWire 800 or 400, and SuperSpeed or Hi-Speed USB.
146	D	FireWire uses serial transmissions, and FireWire devices are hot-swappable.
147	C	To uninstall a USB device such as the USB keyboard, click Uninstall a program in the Control Panel.
148	A	A barcode reader is used to scan barcodes on products at the point of sale (POS) or when taking inventory. The reader might use a wireless connection, a serial port, a USB port, or a keyboard port.
149	C	Fingerprint readers can look like a mouse and use a wireless or USB connection, or they can be embedded on a keyboard, flash drive, or laptop case.
150	D	Using embedded memory or flash memory cards, you can connect the device to your computer using a USB or FireWire port and cable.
151	C	Use the setup CD to install the software and then plug in the webcam to a USB port.
152	A	MIDI standards are used to connect electronic music equipment, such as musical keyboards and mixers, or to connect this equipment to a PC for input, output, and editing.
153	B	As an add-on device, the touch screen has its own AC adapter to power it.
154	B	Switch between computers by using a hot key on the keyboard, buttons on the top of the KVM switch, or a wired remote.
155	C	AGP and PCIe x16 slots use a retention mechanism in the slot to help stabilize a heavy card.
156	A	A graphics tablet, also called a digitizing tablet or digitizer, is used to hand draw and is likely to connect by a USB port.
157	B	For an unstable motherboard, you can try downloading and installing updated chipset drivers and other drivers for onboard components.
158	D	Make sure the replacement battery is an exact match to the original or is one the motherboard manufacturer recommends for the board.
159	A	Beginning with the release in 2006 of the Intel i800 series of chipsets, a hub using the Accelerated Hub Architecture is used to connect buses. This hub has a fast and slow end, and each end is a separate chip on the motherboard.

A

Question	Answer	Explanation
160	B	BitLocker Encryption in Windows 7/Vista is designed to work with a TPM chip; the chip holds the BitLocker encryption key (also called the startup key). If the hard drive is stolen from the computer and installed in another computer, the data would be safe because BitLocker has encrypted all contents on the drive and would not allow access without the startup key stored on the TPM chip.
161	C	BIOS settings might offer several security features. For example, Event Logger allows you to enable event logging, which logs when the case is opened. To use the feature, you must use a cable to connect a switch on the case to a header on the motherboard.
162	B	Boot the PC and enter BIOS setup. If BIOS setup has the option to select the order in which video cards are initialized, verify that the currently installed card is configured to initialize first.
163	D	A local printer connects directly to a computer by way of a USB port, parallel port, serial port, or wireless connection (Bluetooth, infrared, or Wi-Fi).
164	B	A network printer has an Ethernet port to connect directly to the network or uses Wi-Fi to connect to a wireless access point.
165	C	Modem cards in desktop computers provide two phone jacks, called RJ-11 jacks, so that one can be used for dial-up networking and the other jack can be used to plug in an extension telephone.
166	D	Installing a new file system on a device is called formatting the device, and the process erases all data on the device.
167	A	Several print jobs can accumulate in the queue; this process is called spooling. To manage the printer queue, double-click the printer icon in the Windows 7 Devices and Printers window.
168	C	After a printer is installed, use the printer Properties box to manage printer features and hardware devices installed on the printer.
169	D	A parallel port is sometimes called a Centronics port, named after the 36-pin Centronics connection used by printers.
170	D	If you have a problem with the installation that is using a parallel port, consider that the port might not be configured correctly in BIOS setup or that there is a problem with the parallel cable.
171	B	If the processor requests something from a slow device and the device is not ready, the device issues a wait state, which is a command to the processor to wait for slower devices to catch up.
172	A	A chipset is a set of chips on the motherboard that works closely with the processor to collectively control the memory, buses on the motherboard, and some peripherals.

Question	Answer	Explanation
173	B	The chipset sends out a continuous pulsating electrical signal on one line of the system bus. This one system clock line, dedicated to carrying the pulse, is read by other components on the motherboard (including the processor, bus slots, memory slots, and so forth) and ensures that all activities are synchronized.
174	D	The speed of memory, Front Side Bus, processor, or other component is measured in hertz (Hz), which is one cycle per second; megahertz (MHz), which is one million cycles per second; and gigahertz (GHz), which is one billion cycles per second. Common ratings for memory are 1333 MHz and 1866 MHz. Common ratings for Front Side Buses are 2600 MHz, 2000 MHz, 1600 MHz, 1333 MHz, 1066 MHz, 800 MHz, 533 MHz, or 400 MHz. A CPU operates from 166 MHz to almost 4 GHz.
175	C	The width of a data bus is called the data path size. Some buses have data paths that are 8, 16, 32, 64, 128, or more bits wide.

DOMAIN 2.0 NETWORKING

Question	Answer	Explanation
1	C	Most communication between computers on a network or the Internet uses the client/server model.
2	D	The methods and rules used for communication are called protocols.
3	B	Packets contain data (called the payload) and information at the beginning of the packet (called the IP header).
4	B	Before data is transmitted on a network, it is first broken up into segments.
5	C	A gateway is any device or computer that network traffic can use to leave one network and go to a different network.
6	C	Every network adapter has a 48-bit (6-byte) number hard-coded on the card by its manufacturer that is unique for that device. The number is written in hex and is called the MAC (Media Access Control) address.
7	A	A router is a device that manages traffic between two or more networks and can help find the best path for traffic to get from one network to another.
8	A	A local area network (LAN) is a network bound by routers or other gateway devices.
9	B	Computers on the same LAN use MAC addresses to communicate.
10	C	Computers on different LANs use IP addresses to communicate over the Internet.

A

Question	Answer	Explanation
11	D	An IP address is a 32-bit or 128-bit string that is assigned to a network connection when the connection is first made.
12	B	An intranet is any private network that uses TCP/IP protocols.
13	A	When several local networks are tied together in a subsystem of the larger intranet, this group of small local networks is called a subnetwork or subnet.
14	C	Each client and server application installed on a computer listens at a predetermined address that uniquely identifies the application on the computer. This address is a number and is called a port number, port, or port address.
15	C	A dynamic IP address is assigned by a server each time it connects to the network.
16	D	A DHCP (dynamic host configuration protocol) server gives an IP address to a computer when it first attempts to initiate a connection to the network and requests an IP address.
17	A	A computer or other device (such as a network printer) that requests an address from a DHCP server is called a DHCP client.
18	C	The Internet Assigned Numbers Authority (IANA at iana.org) is responsible for keeping track of assigned IP addresses and has already released all its available 32-bit IP addresses.
19	D	When data is routed over the Internet, the network portion of the IP address is used to locate the right network.
20	B	Class B networks range from 128.0.x.y to 191.255.x.y.
21	C	Class C networks range from 192.0.0.x to 223.255.255.x.
22	D	Class D addresses begin with octets 224 through 239 and are used for multicasting.
23	C	IP address 127.0.0.1 indicates your own computer and is called the loopback address.
24	A	A subnet mask is a string of ones followed by a string of zeros. The ones in a subnet mask say, "On our network, this part of an IP address is the network part," and the group of zeros says, "On our network, this part of an IP address is the host part."
25	C	The subnet mask used with IPv4 identifies which part of an IP address is the network portion and which part is the host portion.
26	B	For two IP addresses to be in the same subnet, the first two octets and the first four bits of the third octet must match.
27	D	The IP addresses available to the Internet are called public IP addresses.

Question	Answer	Explanation
28	B	NAT is a TCP/IP protocol that substitutes the public IP address of the router for the private IP address of the other computer when these computers need to communicate on the Internet.
29	B	Internet standards are proposed to the networking community in the form of an RFC (Request for Comment).
30	C	A link, sometimes called the local link, is a local area network (LAN) or wide area network (WAN) bounded by routers.
31	D	An interface is a node's attachment to a link.
32	B	The last 64 bits or 4 blocks of an IP address identify the interface and are called the interface ID or interface identifier.
33	A	If a computer first connects to the network and is unable to lease an IP address from the DHCP server, it uses an Automatic Private IP Address (APIPA) in the address range 169.254.x.y.
34	A	Three tunneling protocols have been developed for IPv6 packets to travel over an IPv4 network: ISATAP, Teredo, and 6TO4.
35	D	A unicast address identifies a single interface on a network.
36	D	Using IPv6, a subnet is, therefore, identified as one or more links that have the same 64 bits in the IP address prefix. This definition implies that a local link is itself a subnet.
37	A	Most global addresses begin with the prefix 2000::/3, although other prefixes are being released.
38	D	Most multicast addresses use the address prefix FF00::/8.
39	B	A domain name identifies a network.
40	A	The process of associating a character-based name with an IP address is called name resolution.
41	B	For TCP to guarantee delivery, it uses IP protocols to establish a session between client and server to verify that communication has taken place.
42	B	HTTPS is used by web browsers and servers to encrypt the data before it is sent and then decrypt it before the data is processed.
43	B	The Secure Shell (SSH) protocol is used to pass login information to a remote computer and control that computer over a network.
44	A	The FTP client receives data on port 20 from the FTP server.
45	C	A DNS server listens at port 53.
46	B	An email client using IMAP receives email at port 143.
47	B	An email client using POP3 receives email at port 110.

A

Question	Answer	Explanation
48	A	As a router, it (SOHO router) stands between the ISP network and the local network routing traffic between the two networks.
49	A	The speed of a network depends on the speed of each device on the network and how well a router manages that traffic.
50	C	Port filtering is used to open or close certain ports so they can or cannot be used.
51	B	Port triggering opens a port when a PC on the network initiates communication through another port.
52	A	When using port forwarding or port triggering, you must lease a static IP address from your ISP so that people on the Internet can find you. Most ISPs will provide you a static IP address for an additional monthly fee.
53	A	If you are having problems getting port forwarding or port triggering to work, putting your computer in a DMZ can free it to receive any communication from the Internet.
54	D	IEEE 802.11n has the following characteristics: • Speeds up to 500 Mbps depending on the configuration • Indoor range up to 70 meters and outdoor range up to 250 meters • Can use either 5.0 GHz or 2.4 GHz radio frequency
55	B	IEEE 802.11b has the following characteristics: • Speeds up to 11 Mbps with a range of up to 100 meters (Indoor ranges are less than outdoor ranges.) • Interference from cordless phones and microwaves in the radio frequency of 2.4 GHz
56	C	If your network must support older 802.11 b/g wireless devices, you must support the 2.4 GHz frequency.
57	B	WPA (Wi-Fi Protected Access), also called TKIP (Temporal Key Integrity Protocol) encryption, is stronger than WEP and was designed to replace it.
58	B	A LAN (local area network) covers a small local area such as a home, office, other building, or small group of buildings.
59	D	A wireless LAN (WLAN) covers a limited geographical area, and is popular in places where networking cables are difficult to install, such as outdoors, in public places, and in homes that are not wired for networks.
60	A	A PAN (personal area network) consists of personal devices communicating at close range such as a cell phone and notebook computer.
61	A	The physical arrangement of the connections between computers is called the network topology or the physical topology.

Question	Answer	Explanation
62	D	When several wireless computers each set up their own ad hoc mode network, the group of networked computers are a mesh network.
63	B	When a star network uses multiple switches in sequence, the switches form a bus network, and the network topology is called a star bus network or a hybrid network.
64	C	A star network uses a centralized device to manage traffic on the network
65	A	By default, an ad hoc network is deleted after you, or all users, disconnect from the network.
66	A	Bandwidth is the theoretical number of bits that can be transmitted over a network at one time, similar to the number of lanes on a highway.
67	C	Latency is measured by the round-trip time it takes for a data packet to travel from source to destination and back to source.
68	D	2G EDGE or 2G E cellular technology has maximum speeds of up to 230 Kbps.
69	B	3G cellular technology uses either CDMA or GSM mobile phone services.
70	A	Broadband refers to a networking technology that carries more than one type of signal, such as DSL and telephone or cable Internet and TV.
71	B	The maximum speed of a T3 network is 44 Mbps.
72	D	An 802.16 wireless (WiMAX) network ranges up to six miles and is used to provide wireless access to an ISP in rural areas.
73	C	10-gigabit Ethernet (10GBaseT) technology is the newest Ethernet standard expected to largely replace SONET, OC, and ATM because of its speed, simplicity, and lower cost.
74	B	DSL uses ordinary copper phone lines and a range of frequencies on the copper wire that are not used by voice, making it possible for you to use the same phone line for voice and DSL at the same time.
75	A	One disadvantage of satellite is that it requires line-of-sight connectivity without obstruction from mountains, trees, and tall buildings.
76	A	WiMAX is sometimes used as a last-mile solution for DSL and cable Internet technologies, which means that the DSL or cable connection goes into a central point in an area, and WiMAX is used for the final leg to the consumer.
77	C	GSM (Global System for Mobile Communications) is an open standard that uses digital communication of data, and is accepted and used worldwide.
78	B	A cellular network or cellular WAN consists of cells, and each cell is controlled by a base station.

A

Question	Answer	Explanation
79	D	The ability to use your cell phone to browse the web, stream music and video, play online games, and use instant messaging and video conferencing is called 2G, 3G, or 4G.
80	A	A PC makes a direct connection to a local wired network by way of a network adapter.
81	D	An example of a MAC address is 00-0C-6E-4E-AB-A5.
82	B	A wired network adapter might provide indicator lights on the side of the RJ-45 port that indicate connectivity and activity.
83	C	A network adapter might support Wake-on-LAN, which allows the adapter to wake up the computer when it receives certain communication on the network.
84	A	Quality of Service (QoS) is the feature of a network adapter that provides the ability to control which applications have priority on the network.
85	B	Using Power over Ethernet (PoE), you can place a wireless access point, webcam, IP phone, or other device that needs power in a position in a building where you don't have an electrical outlet.
86	D	Phone cords are a type of twisted-pair cable and use an RJ-11 connector.
87	A	Modem cards in desktop computers provide two phone jacks, called RJ-11 jacks, so that one can be used for dial-up networking and the other jack can be used to plug in an extension telephone.
88	C	Just before a packet is put on the network, the network adapter adds additional information to the beginning and end of the packet, and this information includes the source and destination MAC addresses. The packet, with this additional information, is now called a frame.
89	B	A hub is just a pass-through and distribution point for every device connected to it, without regard for what kind of data is passing through and where the data might be going.
90	A	A switch learns the addresses for devices connected to it as the switch receives frames and records the source MAC addresses in its MAC address table.
91	D	A bridge is a device that stands between two segments of a network and manages network traffic between them.
92	A	VoIP (Voice over Internet Protocol) is a TCP/IP protocol that manages voice communication over the Internet.
93	A	A VoIP phone connects directly to a network by way of an Ethernet port or an embedded Ethernet cable.
94	B	The NAS enclosure provides four bays for hard drives and an Ethernet port to connect to the network and supports RAID.

Question	Answer	Explanation
95	A	A VoIP phone uses firmware to configure its TCP/IP settings (including its IP address) and the phone number assigned to the phone.
96	C	An Internet appliance is a type of thin client that is designed to make it easy for a user to connect to the Internet, browse the web, use email, and perform other simple chores on the Internet.
97	B	The maximum cable length of a 10Base2 (ThinNet) cable system is 185 meters or 607 feet.
98	C	The maximum cable length of a 10Base5 (ThickNet) cable system is 500 meters or 1,640 feet.
99	A	The maximum cable length of a 100BaseT (Fast Ethernet) cable system is 100 meters or 328 feet.
100	B	10Base5 (ThickNet) is coaxial and uses an AUI 15-pin D-shaped connector.
101	C	100BaseT (Fast Ethernet) is a twisted pair (UTP or STP) cable that uses an RJ-45 connector.
102	D	100BaseFX is a fiber-optic cable that uses ST or SC connectors or LC and MT-RJ connectors.
103	D	The maximum cable length of a 100BaseFL cable system is up to 2 kilometers (6,562 feet).
104	A	Twisted pair cable comes in two varieties: unshielded twisted pair (UTP) cable and shielded twisted pair (STP) cable.
105	B	STP cable uses a covering or shield around each pair of wires inside the cable that protects it from electromagnetic interference caused by electrical motors, transmitters, or high-tension lines.
106	A	Coaxial cable has a single copper wire down the middle and a braided shield around it.
107	D	RG-6 cables use an F connector.
108	C	Fiber-optic cables transmit signals as pulses of light over glass or plastic strands inside protected tubing.
109	B	Fiber-optic cables can use one of four connectors - two older types are ST (straight tip) connectors and SC (subscriber connector or standard connector) connectors. Two newer types are LC (local connector) connectors and MT-RJ (mechanical transfer registered jack) connectors.
110	C	Gigabit Ethernet is becoming the most popular choice for LAN technology.
111	A	A loopback plug can be used to test a network cable or port.
112	B	You can use a cable tester to locate the ends of a network cable in a building.

A

Question	Answer	Explanation
113	D	A network multimeter can be used to detect the Ethernet speed, duplex status, default router on the network, length of a cable, voltage levels of PoE, and other network statistics and details.
114	C	A toner probe, sometimes called a tone probe, is a two-part kit that is used to find cables in the walls of a building.
115	A	A wire stripper is used to build your own network cable or repair a cable.
116	C	A crimper is used to attach a terminator or connector to the end of a cable.
117	B	A punchdown tool, also called an impact tool, is used to punch individual wires in a network cable into their slots in a keystone RJ-45 jack that is used in an RJ-45 wall jack.
118	A	A patch panel provides multiple network ports for cables that converge in one location such as an electrical closet or server room.
119	A	When terminating a cable in a keystone jack, you first gently push each wire down into the color-coded slot of the keystone jack and then you use the punchdown tool to punch the wire down all the way into the slot.
120	C	For Gigabit Ethernet (1000BaseT) that transmits data on all four pairs, you must not only cross the green and orange pairs but also cross the blue and brown pairs to make a crossover cable.

DOMAIN 3.0 LAPTOPS

Question	Answer	Explanation
1	C	A notebook, also called a laptop, is designed for portability and can be just as powerful as a desktop computer.
2	B	An all-in-one computer has the monitor and computer case built together and uses components that are common to both a notebook and a desktop computer.
3	A	Warranties can be voided by opening the case, removing part labels, installing other-vendor parts, upgrading the OS, or disassembling the system unless directly instructed to do so by the authorized service center help desk personnel.
4	D	A notebook service manual tells you how to use diagnostic tools, troubleshoot a notebook, and replace components
5	A	User manuals might contain directions for upgrading and replacing components that do not require disassembling the case, such as how to upgrade memory or install a new hard drive.

Question	Answer	Explanation
6	C	Most notebook computers come with a recovery partition on the hard drive that contains a copy of the OS build, device drivers, and preinstalled applications needed to restore the system to its factory state.
7	D	When you first become responsible for a notebook, make sure you have recovery discs containing the installed OS so you can recover from a failed hard drive.
8	A	LCD panels on notebooks are fragile and can be damaged fairly easily.
9	B	The Disk Management utility in Windows can be used to see a list of hard drives installed in a system and the partitions on each drive.
10	D	The Fn key and F5 or F6 control the screen brightness on many notebooks.
11	B	The most common pointing device on a notebook is a touchpad.
12	D	IBM and Lenovo ThinkPad notebooks use a unique and popular pointing device embedded in the keyboard called a TrackPoint or pointing stick.
13	A	Most peripheral devices on today's notebooks use a USB port to connect to the notebook.
14	A	PCMCIA cards include one or more variations of PC Card, CardBus, and ExpressCard.
15	C	Three standards for PC Cards and PC Card slots that pertain to size are Type I, Type II, and Type III.
16	B	CardBus slots improved PC Card slots by increasing the bus width to 32 bits, while maintaining backward compatibility with earlier standards.
17	C	An ExpressCard slot is fully hot-pluggable (add a card while the system is on), hot-swappable (exchange or add a card while the system is on), and supports autoconfiguration, just as does a USB port.
18	C	An inverter is an electrical device that changes DC to AC.
19	A	A sheet battery attaches to the bottom of a notebook and adds up to six hours to the battery charge
20	D	If you are using the AC adapter to power your notebook when the power goes out, the installed battery serves as a built-in UPS.
21	B	Hibernation saves all work to the hard drive and powers down the system.
22	A	In S1 state, the hard drive and monitor are turned off and everything else runs normally.
23	C	In S3 state, everything is shut down except RAM and enough of the system to respond to a wake-up.
24	C	S4 state is hibernation.
25	D	S5 state is the power off state after a normal shutdown.

A

Question	Answer	Explanation
26	B	A port replicator provides ports to allow a notebook to easily connect to a full-sized monitor, keyboard, AC power adapter, and other peripheral devices.
27	A	A docking station provides the same functions as a port replicator but provides additional slots for adding secondary storage devices and expansion cards.
28	D	Some notebooks have a connector, called a docking port, on the bottom of the notebook to connect to a port replicator or docking station.
29	A	A hardware profile is a group of settings that Windows keeps about a specific hardware configuration.
30	A	Before you send a notebook for repairs, if possible, back up any important data on the hard drive.
31	A	Ground yourself by using an antistatic ground strap.
32	A	A 2.66" 204-pin SO-DIMM contains DDR3 memory.
33	B	A 2.66" 200-pin SO-DIMM contains DDR2 SDRAM.
34	D	A 2.66" 144-pin SO-DIMM contains SDRAM.
35	A	A 2.35" 72-pin SO-DIMMs contain FPM or EDO memory
36	C	A 160-pin SO-RIMM contains Rambus memory.
37	C	Notebook IDE connectors use 44 pins.
38	D	For IDE drives, some notebooks use an adapter to interface between the 44-pin IDE connector on the hard drive and a proprietary connector on the notebook motherboard.
39	C	If you are upgrading from a low-capacity drive to a higher-capacity drive, you need to consider how you will transfer data from the old drive to the new one. One way to do that is to use a USB-to-IDE or USB-to-SATA converter.
40	A	Before deciding to replace a hard drive, make sure you have the recovery media before you start.
41	B	Before opening the case of a notebook or touching sensitive components, you should always use a ground strap to protect the system against ESD.
42	D	When removing cables, know that sometimes cable connectors are ZIF connectors.
43	B	Reassemble the notebook in the reverse order of the way you disassembled it.
44	C	The steps for removing a DVD drive are: (1) Remove the keyboard. (2) Remove the screw that holds the DVD drive to the notebook. (3) Slide the drive out of the bay. (4) Replace the screw.

Question	Answer	Explanation
45	C	Mini PCI Express slots use 52 pins on the edge connector.
46	B	Mini PCI cards are about twice the size of Mini PCI Express cards
47	A	(1) Disconnect antenna (2) Remove screw (3)Pull and lift card from slot
48	D	By far, the most used AMD mobile socket is the 638-pin S1 socket.
49	C	For many laptops, removing the cover on the bottom of a laptop exposes the processor fan and heat sink assembly.
50	B	Plasma is expected to use only about 20 percent as much power as LCD and gives better quality display than LCD.

DOMAIN 4.0 PRINTERS

Question	Answer	Explanation
1	D	Windows can send the commands and data needed to build a page to the printer using the PostScript language by Adobe Systems.
2	A	PCL was developed by Hewlett-Packard but is considered a de facto standard in the printing industry.
3	C	Windows 7/Vista uses either GDI or XPS for rendering based on the type of printer driver installed.
4	B	A bitmap is just a bunch of bits in rows and columns.
5	A	Each row in the bitmap is called a raster line.
6	D	GDI draws and formats the page, converting it to bitmap form, and then sends the almost-ready-to-print bitmap to the printer.
7	C	Text data that contains no graphics or embedded control characters is sent to the printer as is, and the printer can print it without any processing. The data is called raw data.
8	B	Routine maintenance and troubleshooting are easier and less expensive on single-purpose printers.
9	A	A laser printer is a type of electrophotographic printer that can range from a small, personal desktop model to a large, network printer capable of handling and printing large volumes continuously.
10	A	Laser printers require the interaction of mechanical, electrical, and optical technologies to work.
11	C	The seven steps of laser printing are: (1) Processing the image (2) Charging or conditioning (3) Exposing or writing (4) Developing (5) Transferring (6) Fusing and (7) Cleaning.

A

Question	Answer	Explanation
12	D	One bitmap image is produced for monochrome images. For color images, one bitmap is produced for each of four colors.
13	D	A laser printer can produce better quality printouts than a dot matrix printer, even when printing at the same dpi, because it can vary the size of the dots it prints, creating a sharp, clear image. Hewlett-Packard (HP) calls this technology of varying the size of dots REt (Resolution Enhancement technology).
14	A	When laser printing, the fuser assembly uses heat and pressure to fuse the toner to the paper.
15	B	The toner cartridge needs replacing the most often, followed by the image drum, the fuser cartridge, and the transfer assembly, in order.
16	C	The pickup roller that pushes forward a sheet of paper from the paper tray.
17	B	The separation pad that keeps more than one sheet of paper from moving forward.
18	D	A printer that is able to print on both sides of the paper is called a duplex printer.
19	B	An inkjet printer uses a type of ink-dispersion printing and does not normally provide the high-quality resolution of laser printers.
20	B	An inkjet printer uses a print head that moves across the paper, creating one line of the image with each pass.
21	A	Bubble-jet printers use tubes of ink that have tiny resistors near the end of each tube. These resistors heat up and cause the ink to boil. Then, a tiny air bubble of ionized ink (ink with an electrical charge) is ejected onto the paper.
22	C	A stepper motor moves the print head and ink cartridges across the paper using a belt to move the assembly and a stabilizing bar to control the movement
23	B	Weight and brightness are the two primary ways of measuring paper quality.
24	D	An impact printer creates a printed page by using some mechanism that touches or hits the paper.
25	B	Impact printers use continuous tractor feeds and fanfold paper (also called computer paper) rather than individual sheets of paper.
26	D	Thermal printers use heat to create an image.
27	A	Thermal transfer printers are used to print receipts, bar code labels, clothing labels, or container labels.

Question	Answer	Explanation
28	C	A local printer connects directly to a computer by way of a USB port, parallel port, serial port, or wireless connection (Bluetooth, infrared, or Wi-Fi). Some printers support more than one method.
29	B	A network printer has an Ethernet port to connect directly to the network or uses Wi-Fi to connect to a wireless access point.
30	A	A network printer is identified on the network by its IP address.
31	D	To install a local USB printer, all you have to do is plug in the USB printer and Windows 7/Vista installs the printer automatically.
32	B	To know the IP address of a network printer, direct the printer to print a configuration page, which should include its IP address.
33	C	Use the System window to find out if a 32-bit or 64-bit OS is installed.
34	D	Parallel ports, commonly used by older printers, transmit data in parallel, eight bits at a time.
35	D	Parallel ports fall into three categories: Standard Parallel Port (SPP), Enhanced Parallel Port, and Extended Capabilities Port.
36	A	Standard Parallel Port (SPP) transmits in only one direction (the computer can communicate with the printer, but the printer cannot communicate with the computer).
37	B	EPP (Enhanced Parallel Port) transmits in both directions.
38	C	A parallel cable has a DB25 connection at the PC end of the cable and a 36-pin Centronics connection at the printer end of the cable.
39	C	Remote users will not be able to use a shared printer if the computer sharing the printer is asleep.
40	A	You can install a shared printer on a remote computer using one of two methods: (1) Use the Windows 7 Devices and Printers window, the Vista Printer window, or the XP Printers and Faxes window, or (2) use Windows Explorer or the Network or My Network Places window.
41	D	Several print jobs can accumulate in the queue, and the process is called spooling.
42	B	Clean the inside of the printer with a dry cloth and remove dust, bits of paper, and stray toner.
43	C	A vacuum cleaner designed to pick up toner is called a toner vacuum.
44	A	An inkjet printer might require calibration to align and/or clean the inkjet nozzles.

A

Question	Answer	Explanation
45	C	Manufacturers of high-end printers provide printer maintenance kits, which include specific printer components, step-by-step instructions for performing maintenance, and any special tools or equipment you need to do maintenance.
46	D	After you have performed the maintenance, be sure to reset the page count so it will be accurate to tell you when you need to do the next routine maintenance.
47	B	Whenever you service the inside of this printer, as a last step always carefully clean the LED erase lamps on the inside of the top cover
48	A	Extra memory can speed up memory performance, reduce print errors, and prevent Out of Memory errors.
49	A	A print server is hardware or software that manages the print jobs sent to one or more printers on a network.
50	A	A print server can be: (1) A dedicated hardware device, (2) software, such as Print Queue Manager by AMT Software, which is installed on a computer on the network, or (3) programs embedded in firmware on a printer, such as HP JetDirect, which is used by many HP printers.

DOMAIN 5.0 OPERATIONAL PROCEDURES

Question	Answer	Explanation
1	B	A volt is a measure of electrical force.
2	A	An amp is a measure of electrical current.
3	C	An ohm is a measure of resistance to electricity.
4	D	A joule is a measure of work or energy.
5	A	A watt is a measure of electrical power.
6	A	Alternating current (AC) goes back and forth, or oscillates, rather than traveling in only one direction.
7	C	Direct current (DC) travels in only one direction and is the type of current that most electronic devices require, including computers.
8	B	A rectifier is a device that converts AC to DC.
9	A	An inverter is a device that converts DC to AC.
10	D	A transformer is a device that changes the ratio of voltage to current.

Question	Answer	Explanation
11	B	Grounding a line means that the line is connected directly to the earth, so that, in the event of a short, the electricity flows into the earth and not back to the power station.
12	A	A ground is the easiest possible path for electricity to follow.
13	B	A capacitor holds its charge even after the power is turned off and the device is unplugged.
14	D	The power supply and monitor are both considered to be a field replaceable unit (FRU).
15	C	Class A extinguishers can use water to put out fires caused by wood, paper, and other combustibles.
16	B	Electrostatic discharge (ESD), commonly known as static electricity, is an electrical charge at rest. When you came indoors, this charge built up on your hair and had no place to go.
17	D	ESD can cause two types of damage in an electronic component: catastrophic failure and upset failure.
18	C	A ground mat, also called an ESD mat, dissipates ESD and is commonly used by bench technicians (also called depot technicians) who repair and assemble computers at their workbenches or in an assembly line.
19	D	Do not work on a computer if you or the computer have just come in from the cold because there is more danger of ESD when the atmosphere is cold and dry.
20	A	A Material Safety Data Sheet (MSDS) explains how to properly handle substances such as chemical solvents and how to dispose of them.
21	B	The steps involved in opening a computer case are: (1) Back up important data (2) Power down the system and unplug it (3) Press and hold down the power button for a moment (4) Have a plastic bag or cup handy to hold screws and (5) Open the case cover.
22	C	When removing an expansion card, lay each expansion card aside on a flat surface, preferably in an antistatic bag.
23	A	The HDD LED connector controls the drive activity light on the front panel that lights up when any SATA or IDE device is in use.
24	B	The power SW connector controls power to the motherboard and must be connected for the PC to power up.
25	C	The positive LED controls the power light and indicates that power is on.
26	A	The negative LED controls the power light, and the two positive and negative leads indicate that power is on.
27	D	The reset SW is the switch used to reboot the computer.

A

Question	Answer	Explanation
28	D	Positive wires connecting the front panel to the motherboard are usually a solid color.
29	B	Negative wires connecting the front panel to the motherboard are usually white or striped.
30	D	A PC support technician is the only one responsible for the PC before trouble occurs.
31	C	An expert system uses databases of known facts and rules to simulate human experts' reasoning and decision making.
32	B	When someone initiates a call for help, the technician starts the process by creating a ticket.
33	A	Part of setting expectations is to establish a timeline with your customer for the completion of a project.
34	C	As you work with a customer on site, avoid distractions.
35	A	Be specific with your instructions. For example, instead of saying, "Open Windows Explorer," say, "Using your mouse, right-click the Start button and select Open Windows Explorer from the menu."
36	B	When you can, compliment the customer's knowledge, experience, or insight.
37	D	When someone purchases software from a software vendor, that person has only purchased a license for the software, which is the right to use it.
38	B	Copyrights are intended to legally protect the intellectual property rights of organizations or individuals to creative works, which include books, images, and software.
39	D	Making unauthorized copies of original software violates the Federal Copyright Act of 1976 and is called software piracy or, more officially, software copyright infringement.
40	C	By purchasing a site license, a company can obtain the right to use multiple copies of software.
41	A	Do not move or jar your desktop computer while the hard drive is working.
42	D	In BIOS setup, disable the ability to write to the boot sector of the hard drive
43	B	An uninterruptible power supply (UPS) is a device that raises the voltage when it drops during brownouts or sags (temporary voltage reductions).
44	B	A UPS also does double-duty as a surge protector to protect the system against power surges or spikes.
45	B	A UPS can provide power for a brief time during a total blackout long enough for you to save your work and shut down the system.

Question	Answer	Explanation
46	A	To completely wipe a hard drive clean without destroying it, you can use a zero-fill utility downloaded from the hard drive manufacturer.
47	C	Dispose of these batteries (AAA, AA, A, C, D, and 9-volt) in the regular trash.
48	A	Button batteries can contain silver oxide, mercury, lithium, or cadmium and are considered hazardous waste. Dispose of them by returning them to the original dealer or by taking them to a recycling center.
49	D	Check with local county or environmental officials for laws and regulations in your area for proper disposal of ink-jet printer cartridges, computer cases, power supplies, and other computer parts.
50	B	Do physical damage to the device (CDs, DVDs, and BDs) so that it is not possible for sensitive data to be stolen.

A

Domain 1.0 Operating Systems

Question	Answer	Explanation
1	D	When two computers communicate using a local network or the Internet, communication happens at three levels (hardware, operating system, and application).
2	A	The first step in communication is that one computer must find the other computer.
3	C	Most communication between computers on a network or the Internet uses this client/server model.
4	B	For almost all networks today, including the Internet, the group or suite of protocols used is called TCP/IP (Transmission Control Protocol/Internet Protocol).
5	D	Before data is transmitted on a network, it is first broken up into segments. Each data segment is put into a packet.
6	D	Three ways Windows supports accessing resources on a network are to use a Windows homegroup, workgroup, or domain.
7	A	A Windows domain is a logical group of networked computers that share a centralized directory database of user account information and security for the entire group of computers.
8	C	For wired networks, the four speeds for Ethernet are 10 Mbps, 100 Mbps (Fast Ethernet or 100BaseT), 1 Gbps (Gigabit Ethernet or 1000BaseT), and 10 Gbps (10-gigabit Ethernet or 10GBaseT).
9	C	Every network adapter (including a wired or wireless) has a 48-bit (6-byte) identification number, called the MAC address or physical address.
10	D	By far, the most popular client/server applications on the Internet are a browser and web server.

B

Question	Answer	Explanation
11	C	An ActiveX control is a small app or add-on that can be downloaded from a web site along with a web page and is executed by IE to enhance the web page (for example, add animation to the page).
12	A	Use the Privacy tab to block cookies that might invade your privacy or steal your identity.
13	A	A proxy server is a computer that intercepts requests that a browser makes of a server.
14	D	The desktop is the initial screen that is displayed after the user logs on and Windows is loaded.
15	B	The Windows 7 and Vista desktop provides a 3-D user interface called the Aero user interface that gives a glassy appearance and is sometimes called Aero glass.
16	C	Windows 7 Home Basic has limited features and is available only in underdeveloped countries and can only be activated in these countries.
17	C	The simplest way to find out if a system can be upgraded to Windows 7 is to download and run the Windows 7 Upgrade Advisor.
18	C	A backup is an extra copy of a data or software file that you can use if the original file becomes damaged or destroyed.
19	C	For individuals or small organizations, an online backup service such as Carbonite (carbonite.com) or Mozy (mozy.com) is the easiest, most reliable, and most expensive solution.
20	D	The Windows System Protection utility automatically backs up system files and stores them on the hard drive at regular intervals and just before you install software or hardware.
21	B	You can use the System Configuration (Msconfig.exe) utility, which is commonly pronounced "M-S-config," to find out what processes are launched at startup and to temporarily disable a process from loading.
22	C	The Services console (the program file is services.msc) is used to control the Windows and third-party services installed on a system.
23	B	BitLocker Encryption in Windows professional and business editions locks down a hard drive by encrypting the entire Windows volume and any other volume on the drive.
24	A	Windows Defender is antispyware included in Windows 7/Vista.
25	B	The Vista Security Center can be used to confirm Windows Firewall, Windows Update, anti-malware settings, including that of Windows Defender, and other security settings.
26	B	Reinstalling from a standard image or deployment image is much faster than going through the detailed process of removing malware from a system.

Question	Answer	Explanation
27	C	Windows 7 Enterprise includes additional features over Windows 7 Professional. The major additional features are BitLocker Drive Encryption used to encrypt an entire hard drive and support for multiple languages.
28	B	According to Table 7-1, from the available options in the question, Windows 7 Home Basic edition only includes Scheduled backups.
29	D	According to Table 7-1, from the available options in the question, only Windows 7 Ultimate supports multiple languages.
30	B	According to Table 7-1, from the available options in the question, only Windows 7 Professional supports Windows XP Mode.
31	C	The OEM license costs less but can only be installed on a new PC for resale.
32	B	According to Table 7-2, the 32-bit version of Windows 7 Home Basic supports up to 4 GB of memory.
33	B	All data is stored on a hard drive in sectors, sometimes called records.
34	A	Sector markings used to organize the drive are done before it leaves the factory in a process called low-level formatting.
35	C	Today's drive capacities are measured in GB (gigabytes, roughly one million bytes) or TB (terabytes, roughly one trillion bytes).
36	C	For magnetic hard drives, each platter is divided into concentric circles called tracks, and each track is divided into sectors.
37	B	Windows can track up to four partitions on a drive. It keeps a map of these partitions in a partition table stored in the very first sector on the hard drive called the Master Boot Record (MBR).
38	B	A drive can have one, two, or three primary partitions, also called volumes.
39	B	One of the primary partitions can be designated the active partition, which is the bootable partition that the startup BIOS turns to when searching for an operating system to start up.
40	C	Windows 7 and Vista have two levels of command prompt windows: a standard window and an elevated window.
41	D	Type cls and press Enter to clear the window.
42	A	To retrieve the last command you entered, press the up arrow.
43	C	To terminate a command before it is finished, press Ctrl+Break or Ctrl+Pause.
44	B	System File Checker (SFC) protects system files and keeps a cache of current system files in case it needs to refresh a damaged file.
45	D	If an application is locked up and not responding, use Task Manager to end it.

B

Question	Answer	Explanation
46	D	The Tasklist command returns the process identify (PID), which is a number that identifies each running process.
47	A	Use the diskpart command to manage hard drives, partitions, and volumes.
48	C	According to Table 14-2, the diskpart list disk command lists installed hard disk drives.
49	C	According to Table 14-2, the diskpart clean command removes any partition or volume information from the selected disk.
50	D	According to Table 14-2, the diskpart active command makes the selected partition the active partition.
51	C	The Ping (Packet InterNet Groper) command tests connectivity by sending an echo request to a remote computer.
52	B	The Ipconfig (IP configuration) command can display TCP/IP configuration information and refresh the TCP/IP assignments to a connection including its IP address.
53	A	In Vista, the box is labeled the Search box, and in Windows XP, it is labeled the Run box.
54	D	A shortcut icon is a clickable item on the desktop that points to a program you can execute, or to a file or folder.
55	B	If a problem occurs while Windows is installing a device, it automatically launches the Action Center to help find a solution.
56	C	Device Manager (its program file is named devmgmt.msc) is your primary Windows tool for managing hardware.
57	C	Video cards have their own processor called a graphics processing unit (GPU) or visual processing unit (VPU).
58	C	Video cards have their own processor called a graphics processing unit (GPU) or visual processing unit (VPU).
59	C	The primary tool for managing hard drives is Disk Management.
60	D	To open the Disk Management window click Start, type Disk Management or diskmgmt.msc in the search box and press Enter.
61	B	A shell is the portion of an OS that relates to the user and to applications.
62	C	The kernel is responsible for interacting with hardware.
63	B	You can quickly identify a problem with memory or eliminate memory as the source of a problem by using the Windows 7/Vista Memory Diagnostics tool.
64	A	In a command prompt window, enter mdsched.exe and press Enter to launch the Windows 7/Vista Memory Diagnostics tool.

Question	Answer	Explanation
65	B	Remote Desktop gives a user access to a Windows desktop from anywhere on the Internet.
66	B	To turn on the Remote Desktop service, open the System window and click Remote settings in the left pane.
67	C	In addition to a hardware network firewall, a large corporation might use a software firewall, also called a corporate firewall.
68	B	A personal firewall, also called a host firewall, is software installed on a computer to protect this computer.
69	D	A print server is hardware or software that manages the print jobs sent to one or more printers on a network
70	D	Windows 7/Vista Professional and Business editions offer the Print Management utility in the Administrative Tools group of Control Panel.
71	C	The Personalization window lets you personalize the way Windows appears, including the desktop, sounds, mouse action, color themes, and display settings.
72	B	The screen resolution is the number of dots or pixels on the monitor screen expressed as two numbers such as 1680 × 1050.
73	B	If you are installing an OEM (Original Equipment Manufacturer) version of Windows 7, look for a sticker on the outside of the DVD case. This sticker contains the product key and is called the Certificate of Authenticity.
74	A	If your computer is part of a Windows domain, when Windows starts up, it displays a blank screen instead of a logon screen. To log onto the domain, press Ctrl+Alt+Del to display the logon screen.
75	C	In order to make sure a valid Windows license has been purchased for each installation of Windows, Microsoft requires product activation.
76	C	DirectX is a Microsoft software development tool that software developers can use to write multimedia applications such as games, video-editing software, and computer-aided design software.
77	B	You can use the dxdiag.exe command to display information about hardware and diagnose problems with DirectX.
78	B	For Windows to enable the Aero user interface, the video controller must have available at least 128 MB video memory.
79	B	When a user first logs onto Windows 7/Vista, a user profile is created, which is a collection of user data and settings.
80	C	In general, a namespace is a container to hold data, for example, a folder.
81	D	Connect a network cable to the Ethernet port (called an RJ-45 port).

B

Question	Answer	Explanation
82	A	A default gateway is the gateway a computer uses to access another network if it does not have a better option.
83	C	A wireless network is created by a wireless device known as the wireless access point.
84	B	Some web servers use the HTTP with SSL or TLS protocols to secure transmissions to and from the web server.
85	D	Use the Internet Options box to manage Internet Explorer settings.
86	D	If you want to delete your browsing history each time you close Internet Explorer, check Delete browsing history on exit on the General tab.
87	A	If you need to configure Internet Explorer to use a specific proxy server, on the Connections tab, click LAN settings.
88	C	In Vista, you can allow exceptions to Windows Firewall by program name or port number.
89	C	The UAC box is one of your best defenses against malware installing itself.
90	D	Network-monitoring software (for example, Big Brother Professional at www.bb4.com) is constantly monitoring the network for unusual activity.
91	C	The most common pointing device on a notebook is a touchpad.
92	B	IBM and Lenovo ThinkPad notebooks use a unique and popular pointing device embedded in the keyboard called a TrackPoint or pointing stick.
93	A	As with all computer problems, begin troubleshooting by interviewing the user, finding out what works and doesn't work, and making an initial determination of the problem.
94	D	To eliminate the printer as the problem, first check that the printer is on, and then print a printer self-test page by using controls at the printer.
95	B	Device Manager (its program file is named devmgmt.msc) is your primary Windows 7/Vista/XP tool for managing hardware.
96	C	Using Device Manager, you can disable or enable a device, update its drivers, uninstall a device, and undo a driver update (called a driver rollback).
97	C	Three Windows settings are critical for keeping the system protected from malware and hackers: Windows Updates, antivirus software, and network location.
98	C	For best performance, Windows needs about 15 percent free space on the hard drive.
99	C	The system image or Complete PC backup is a backup of the Windows volume and is called a recovery image.

Question	Answer	Explanation
100	D	Windows XP can make a backup of the entire Windows volume using the Automated System Recovery tool.
101	B	To boot to the network, go into BIOS setup and set the first boot device to be Ethernet. The PC then boots to the Pre-Execution Environment (PXE) and then PXE searches for a server on the network for Windows PE and the deployment image.
102	C	These snapshots of the system are called restore points and include Windows system files that have changed since the last restore point was made.
103	B	To make sure System Protection has not been turned off, open the System window and click System protection.
104	A	Restore points are normally kept in the folder C:\System Volume Information, which is not accessible to the user.
105	B	Wake on LAN (WoL) causes the host computer to turn on even from a powered-off state when a specific type of network activity happens.
106	B	Wake on LAN must be supported by your motherboard and network adapter and must be enabled in both Windows and BIOS setup.
107	C	The Group Policy utility controls what users can do with a system and how the system is used and is available with business and professional editions of Windows.
108	B	Using Group Policy, you can set security policies to help secure a workstation.
109	D	Using client-side virtualization, a personal computer provides multiple virtual environments for applications.
110	D	Using presentation virtualization, a remote application running on a server is controlled by a local computer.
111	C	Using application virtualization, a virtual environment is created in memory for an application to virtually install itself.
112	B	Using client-side desktop virtualization, software installed on a desktop or laptop manages virtual machines.
113	B	Windows Virtual PC and Oracle VirtualBox are two examples of freeware that can be installed on a computer and used to manage virtual machines. This type of software is called a hypervisor or virtual machine manager (VMM).
114	A	Software used to create and manage virtual machines on a server or on a local computer is called a virtual machine manager (VMM) or hypervisor.
115	A	A Type 1 hypervisor installs on a computer before any operating system, and is, therefore, called a bare-metal hypervisor.

B

DOMAIN 2.0 SECURITY

Question	Answer	Explanation
1	B	Quality of Service (QoS) can improve network performance for an application by raising its priority for allotted network bandwidth.
2	D	To configure Windows to provide QoS for applications, you must enable QoS for the network connection and adapter.
3	C	Group Policy (gpedit.msc) is a console available only in Windows professional and business editions.
4	A	Group Policy works by making entries in the registry, applying scripts to Windows startup, shutdown, and logon processes, and affecting security settings.
5	D	Computer-based polices are applied just before the logon screen appears.
6	B	User-based policies are applied after logon.
7	A	The priority level is determined by a DSCP (Differentiated Services Code Point) value, which is a number from 0 to 63. The higher the number, the higher the priority.
8	C	To apply a new policy, you can restart the computer or enter gpupdate.exe at a command prompt.
9	B	Rights (also called privileges) refer to the tasks an account is allowed to do in the system (for example, installing software or changing the system date and time).
10	D	Rights (also called privileges) refer to the tasks an account is allowed to do in the system (for example, installing software or changing the system date and time).
11	C	Permissions refer to which user accounts or user groups are allowed access to data files and folders.
12	A	Rights are assigned to an account, and permissions are assigned to data files and folders.
13	A	You, as the support technician, will be responsible to make sure the user account assigned to the employee has these rights and no more. This approach is called the principle of least privilege.
14	D	User accounts can be assigned to different user groups using the Computer Management console (using business and professional editions of Windows).
15	B	An administrator account has complete access to the system and can make changes that affect the security of the system and other users.
16	C	A standard user account is sometimes called a user account.

Question	Answer	Explanation
17	A	Windows XP offers two account types for new accounts: an administrator account and a limited account.
18	C	By default, administrator accounts belong to the Administrators group.
19	B	By default, standard user accounts belong to the Users group.
20	D	The Guests group has limited rights on the system and is given a temporary profile that is deleted when the user logs off.
21	B	An account in the Backup Operators group can back up and restore any files on the system regardless of its access permissions to these files.
22	D	Windows XP has a Power Users group that can read from and write to parts of the system other than its own user profile folders, install applications, and perform limited administrative tasks.
23	B	The Authenticated Users group includes all user accounts that can access the system except the Guest account.
24	A	When you share a file or folder on the network or to a homegroup, by default, Windows gives access to the Everyone group.
25	B	Anonymous users are those users who have not been authenticated on a remote computer.
26	A	Using the Management Console in business and professional editions of Windows, you can create your own user groups.
27	C	When all users on a network require the same access to all resources, you can use a Windows homegroup.
28	D	After the homegroup is set up, to share a file or folder with the homegroup, use the Sharing Wizard.
29	D	For better security than a homegroup, use workgroup sharing. Using this method, you decide which users on the network have access to which shared folder and the type of access they have.
30	B	A file server is a computer dedicated to storing and serving up data files and folders.
31	C	Private data for individual users is best kept in the C:\Users folder.
32	A	The C:\Users\Public folder is intended to be used for folders and files that all users share.
33	B	Using workgroup sharing, Windows offers two methods to share a folder over the network: share permissions and NTFS permissions.
34	A	Share permissions grant permissions only to network users.
35	D	Share permissions work on NTFS, FAT32, and exFAT volumes.

B

Question	Answer	Explanation
36	C	NTFS permissions apply to local users and network users and apply to both folders and individual files.
37	B	Permission propagation is when permissions are passed from parent to child.
38	C	Inherited permissions are permissions that are attained from a parent object.
39	A	You can use the xcopy or robocopy command with switches to change the rules for how inherited permissions are managed when copying and moving files.
40	B	When you move or copy an object to a folder, the object takes on the permissions of that folder.
41	B	By default, when you share a folder in Windows XP, it is shared with everyone because XP uses simple file sharing.
42	D	For Windows XP to share resources, two services, Client for Microsoft Networks and File and Printer Sharing for Microsoft Networks, must be installed and enabled for the network connection.
43	C	Permissions that are manually set are called explicit permissions.
44	A	A network drive map makes one computer (the client) appear to have a new hard drive, such as drive E, that is really hard drive space on another host computer (the server).
45	D	A network-attached storage (NAS) device provides hard drive storage for computers on a network.
46	B	Network File System (NFS), which makes it possible for files on the network to be accessed as easily as if they are stored on the local computer.
47	A	If you want to share a folder, but don't want others to see the shared folder in Windows Explorer, add a $ to the end of the folder name. This shared and hidden folder is called a hidden share.
48	C	Folders and files on a computer that are shared with others on the network using local user accounts are called local shares.
49	B	Administrative shares are folders that are shared by default that administrator accounts at the domain level can access.
50	D	The admin$ administrative share is called the Remote Admin share.
51	C	A user is authenticated when he proves he is who he says he is.
52	A	Normally, Windows authenticates a user with a Windows password.
53	A	A more secure method of logon is to require the user to press Ctrl+Alt+Delete to get to a logon window.
54	D	Use the netplwiz command to change the way Windows logon works.

Question	Answer	Explanation
55	B	Generally speaking, the weakest link in setting up security in a computer environment is people.
56	C	Social engineering is the practice of tricking people into giving out private information or allowing unsafe programs into the network or computer.
57	D	Be aware of shoulder surfing when other people secretly peek at your monitor screen as you work.
58	A	Users need to be on the alert for tailgating, which is when someone who is unauthorized follows the employee through a secured entrance to a room or building.
59	C	Another form of tailgating is when a user steps away from her computer and another person continues to use the Windows session when the system is not properly locked.
60	B	Phishing (pronounced "fishing") is a type of identity theft where the sender of an email message scams you into responding with personal data about yourself.
61	C	Malicious software is any unwanted program that means you harm and is transmitted to your computer without your knowledge.
62	D	Malicious software is also called malware.
63	A	Grayware is any annoying and unwanted program that might or might not mean you harm.
64	B	A virus is a program that replicates by attaching itself to other programs.
65	D	A boot sector virus is a virus that hides in the MBR program in the boot sector of a hard drive or in an OS boot loader program.
66	B	A keylogger tracks all your keystrokes and can be used to steal a person's identity, credit card numbers, Social Security number, bank information, passwords, email addresses, and so forth.
67	A	A worm is a program that copies itself throughout a network or the Internet without a host program.
68	C	A Trojan does not need a host program to work; rather, it substitutes itself for a legitimate program.
69	A	A rootkit is a virus that loads itself before the OS boot is complete.
70	B	To keep a system secure, users need to practice the habit of locking down their workstation each time they step away from their desks. The quickest way to do this is to press the Windows key + L.
71	C	A password needs to be a strong password, which means it should not be easy to guess by both humans and computer programs designed to hack passwords.

B

Question	Answer	Explanation
72	C	For strong passwords use eight or more characters (14 characters or longer is better).
73	D	The Properties box for many policies offers the Explain tab. Use this tab to read more about a policy and how it works.
74	B	To find out the resulting policies for the computer or user that are currently applied to the system, you can use the Gpresult command in a command prompt window with parameters.
75	A	The group of policies in the Local Computer Policy, Computer Configuration, Windows Settings, Security Settings group can also be edited from the Control Panel. In the Control Panel, open the Administrative Tools and double-click Local Security Policy.
76	C	You can perform a low-level format of a drive to overwrite the data with zeroes.
77	B	A degausser exposes a storage device to a strong magnetic field to completely erase the data on a magnetic hard drive or tape drive.
78	A	The American National Standards Institute (ANSI) developed the ATA Secure Erase standards for securely erasing data from solid state devices such as a USB flash drive or SSD drive. Degaussing does not erase data on a solid state hard drive or other flash media because these devices don't use a magnetic surface to hold data.
79	B	For the very best data destruction, consider a secure data-destruction service.
80	C	It's extremely important to protect access to your network and prevent others from hijacking your router. Change the default password to your router firmware. If the firmware offers the option, disable the ability to configure the router from over the wireless network.

DOMAIN 3.0 MOBILE DEVICES

Question	Answer	Explanation
1	D	The Android operating system is based on the Linux OS and uses a Linux kernel. Linux and Android are open source, which means the source code for the operating system is available for free and anyone can modify and redistribute the source code.
2	B	Releases of Android are named after desserts and include Froyo or frozen yogurt (version 2.2.x), Gingerbread (version 2.3.x), Honeycomb (version 3.x), and Ice Cream Sandwich (version 4.x).

Question	Answer	Explanation
3	A	On Android phones, up to four apps can be pinned to the dock at the bottom of the screen.
4	C	Android apps are sold or freely distributed from any source or vendor. However, the official source for apps, called the Android marketplace, is Google Play at play.google.com.
5	A	Most Android apps are written using the Java programming language.
6	D	Apple iPhone (a smartphone), iPad (a handheld tablet), and iPod touch (a multimedia recorder and player and a game player). These devices all use the iOS operating system, also developed and owned by Apple. The iOS is based on OS X, the operating system used by Apple desktop and laptop computers.
7	B	As Apple is the sole developer and manufacturer, it can maintain strict standards on its products, which means the iOS is extremely stable and bug free. The iOS is also a very easy and intuitive operating system to use. The iOS can have up to 11 home screens.
8	C	The only place to go for an iOS app is Apple. Apple is the sole distributer of iOS apps at its iTunes App Store (itunes.apple.com).
9	C	Apple is the sole distributer of iOS apps at its iTunes App Store (itunes.apple.com). Other developers can write apps for the iPhone, iPad, or iPod, but these apps must be sent to Apple for their close scrutiny. If they pass muster, they are distributed by Apple on its web site. One requirement is that an app be written in the Objective-C, C, or C++ programming language.
10	D	A touch screen that can handle a two-finger pinch is called a multitouch screen.
11	C	The internal storage used by Android and iOS for their apps and data is a solid state device (SSD), a type of flash memory.
12	A	A gyroscope is a device that contains a disc that is free to move and can respond to gravity as the device is moved.
13	C	A smartphone can determine its position by using the GPS satellite data or data from the position of nearby cellular towers in its cellular network.
14	A	A mobile device routinely reports its position to Apple or Google at least twice a day, and usually more often, which makes it possible for these companies to track your device's whereabouts, which is called geotracking.
15	D	The accelerometer is used by the OS and apps to adjust the screen orientation from portrait to landscape as the user rotates the device.
16	C	The devices might require a Bluetooth PIN code to complete the Bluetooth connection.

B

Question	Answer	Explanation
17	A	Using a personal computer or mobile device, email can be managed in one of two ways: • Use a browser. Using a browser, go to the web site of your email provider and manage your email on the web site. • Use an email client. An email client, such as Microsoft Outlook, can be installed on your personal computer, or you can use an email app on your mobile device.
18	D	This server will use POP or IMAP. Using IMAP, you are managing your email on the server.
19	A	A POP server uses port 110 unless it is secured and using SSL.
20	B	Normally, when you use the Mail app, you can delete a message by selecting it and tapping Delete. However, using Gmail, by default, you archive a message rather than delete it.
21	D	For Apple devices, you can back up app data, iOS settings, email, contacts, wallpaper, and multimedia content, including photos, music, and videos, by syncing this content using iTunes or iCloud.
22	A	When you sync the content of Apple devices with iTunes, the backup is stored on your computer at this location using Windows 7/Vista: C:\Users\username\AppData\Roaming\Apple Computer\MobileSync\Backup
23	D	iCloud requires iOS 5 or higher. To configure iCloud, tap Settings, iCloud.
24	D	To protect your device in case it is stolen, you can set a passcode. For iOS devices, tap Settings, General, Passcode Lock, Turn Passcode On, and enter a four-digit code.
25	B	If you decide a device cannot be found, you might want to click Remote Wipe to perform a remote wipe, which remotely erases all contacts, email, photos, and other data from the device to protect your privacy.
26	C	For the purposes of mobile device PC support technicians, there are no field-replaceable units (FRU) in mobile devices, and it is not possible to upgrade or replace internal components. (Although it is possible to replace the screens in some mobile devices, a support technician is not expected to have this skill.) SIM cards and batteries can be replaced, and accessories such as a battery charger or ear buds can be attached.
27	A	Most of the settings you need to support an Android device are found in the Settings app.
28	D	Restoring data and settings from backup can be quite a production because no one app backs up all the data on an Android device.

Question	Answer	Explanation
29	B	To set a passcode for an Android, tap Settings, Location & security. On the Location & security screen, tap Configure lock screen. On the next screen, you can set a pattern, PIN, or password that must be entered to unlock the device. A pattern is the most secure, which requires you to use your finger to connect at least four dots on the screen.
30	A	Rooting is the process of obtaining root or administrator privileges to an Android device, which then gives you complete access to the entire file system (all folders and files) and all commands and features.

DOMAIN 4.0 TROUBLESHOOTING

Question	Answer	Explanation
1	B	If you have a problem that prevents the PC from booting that you suspect is related to hardware, you can install the POST card in an expansion slot on the motherboard and then attempt to boot. The card monitors the boot process and reports errors, usually as coded numbers on a small LED panel on the card.
2	C	The first step in a systematic method for troubleshooting is to interview the user and back up data before you make any changes to the system.
3	B	Follow Rule 8: Divide and Conquer. You can use one or more of the following to help you divide and conquer on your own system: • In Windows, stop all nonessential services running in the background to eliminate them as the problem. • Boot from a bootable CD or DVD to eliminate the OS and startup files on the hard drive as the problem. • Start Windows in Safe Mode to eliminate unnecessary startup programs as a source of the problem
4	D	Good documentation helps you take what you learned into the next troubleshooting situation, train others, develop effective preventive maintenance plans, and satisfy any audits or customer or employer queries about your work.
5	A	A blue screen error, also called a stop error or a blue screen of death (BSOD), happens when processes running in kernel mode encounter a problem and Windows must stop the system.
6	D	NTFS_FILE_SYSTEM indicates that the hard drive is most likely corrupted. Try running Chkdsk with the /r parameter.
7	B	KERNEL_DATA_INPAGE_ERROR indicates that Windows could not read the paging file (Pagefile.sys).

B

Question	Answer	Explanation
8	C	UNEXPECTED_KERNEL_MODE_TRAP is most likely caused by bad memory.
9	A	DIVIDE_BY_ZERO_ERROR is most likely caused by an application.
10	B	The term x86 refers to 32-bit CPUs or processors and to 32-bit operating systems.
11	D	All CPUs installed in personal computers today are hybrid processors that can process either 32 bits or 64 bits.
12	C	System File Checker (SFC) protects system files and keeps a cache of current system files in case it needs to refresh a damaged file.
13	A	Improper shutdowns and a system lockup that cause a computer to freeze and require a restart are most likely caused by hardware.
14	C	Check Event Viewer to see if it has reported a hardware failure.
15	D	To boot to Safe Mode, press F8 before Windows loads.
16	A	For Windows 7, the Action Center tracks problems with applications, hardware, and Windows.
17	C	The Event Viewer logs might give clues about applications and the system.
18	A	For essential hardware devices, use System File Checker (SFC) to verify and replace system files.
19	C	If you can identify the approximate date the error started and that date is in the recent past, use System Restore.
20	D	The Taskkill command uses the process ID to kill the process.
21	A	The file association between a data file and an application is determined by the file extension.
22	C	If a file extension is not listed in the Set Associations window, the Data Sources Open Database Connectivity (ODBC) tool in the Administrative Tools group of Control Panel can help. This tool can be used to allow data files (called data sources) to be connected to applications they normally would not use.
23	D	A service can be disabled at startup using the System Configuration tool.
24	B	If you get an error message that a service has failed to start, check the Service console to make sure the service is set to start automatically. Make sure the Startup type is set to Automatic or Automatic (Delayed Start). Use the service's Properties box in the console to find the path and filename to the executable program.

Question	Answer	Explanation
25	A	If the application has never worked, follow these steps: 1. Update Windows and search the web 2. Run the installation program or application as an administrator
26	D	Although applications that are not digitally signed can still run on Windows, a digital signature does verify that the application is not a rogue application and that it is certified as Windows-compatible by Microsoft.
27	C	User manuals often list error messages and their meanings.
28	B	If a system shuts down unexpectedly, try to find out what was happening at the time of the shutdowns to zero in on an application or device causing the problem. Possible sources of the problem are an overheating or faulty RAM, motherboard, or processor.
29	C	Startup BIOS communicates POST errors as a series of beeps before it tests video.
30	A	Consider smoke or a burning smell as a serious electrical problem. Immediately unplug the computer.
31	D	When a fan spins but no power gets to other devices, begin by checking the power supply. Are connectors securely connected? Use a power supply tester to check for correct voltage outputs.
32	A	An easy way to temporarily install a hard drive in a system is to use a USB port.
33	B	If the hard drive has important data on it that has not been backed up, your first priority is most likely to recover the data.
34	D	If the power supply is grossly inadequate, the computer's electrical system will whine when you first plug up the power.
35	C	A short might occur if some component on the motherboard makes improper contact with the chassis.
36	A	Overheating can cause intermittent errors, the system to hang, or components to fail or not last as long as they normally would.
37	D	If you suspect overheating, know that processors can sense their operating temperatures and report that information to BIOS.
38	A	If the system refuses to boot or hangs after a period of activity, suspect overheating.
39	C	For better ventilation, use a power supply that has vents on the bottom and front of the power supply.
40	D	Intel and AMD both recommend a chassis air guide (CAG) as part of the case design.

B

Question	Answer	Explanation
41	B	Error messages on the screen indicate that video and the electrical system are working.
42	C	One short beep or no beep indicates that the computer passed all POST tests.
43	D	One long and one short beep during POST indicate a motherboard problem.
44	A	One long and three short beeps during POST indicate a video problem.
45	B	Three long beeps during POST indicate a keyboard controller problem.
46	D	Continuous high and low beeps indicate a CPU problem.
47	D	To disable automatic restarts, press F8 as Windows starts up. The Advanced Boot Options menu appears.
48	A	The field replaceable units (FRUs) on a motherboard are the processor, the processor cooler assembly, RAM, and the CMOS battery.
49	C	In Windows, the best tool to check for potential hardware problems is Device Manager.
50	A	If you cannot load the Windows desktop, press the Spacebar during the boot. The Windows Boot Manager screen appears.
51	C	When you first install a device, Windows stores a copy of the driver software in a driver store.
52	C	The Power Switch lead from the front of the case must be connected to the header on the motherboard.
53	B	Spacers installed in case holes keep the motherboard from causing a short.
54	C	Hardware problems usually show up at POST, unless there is physical damage to an area of the hard drive that is not accessed during POST.
55	A	For a RAID array, use the firmware utility to check the status of each disk in the array and to check for errors.
56	B	Regardless of how an enclosure connects to a computer or network, the hard drives inside the enclosure might use a SATA or PATA connection.
57	D	A Green motherboard (one that follows energy-saving standards) used with an Energy Saver monitor can be configured to go into standby or sleep mode after a period of inactivity.
58	B	An LCD monitor might have pixels that are not working called dead pixels, which can appear as small white, black, or colored spots on your screen.
59	C	A black or white pixel is likely to be a broken transistor that cannot be fixed.
60	B	Horizontally torn images on-screen are called artifacts, and happen when the video feed from the video controller gets out of sync with the refresh of the monitor screen.
61	D	Monitor flicker can be caused by poor cable connections.

Question	Answer	Explanation
62	C	Odd-colored blotches on the screen or a screen flicker might indicate a device such as a speaker or fan is sitting too close to the monitor and emitting electrical noise called electromagnetic interference or EMI.
63	A	Does the monitor have a degauss button to eliminate accumulated or stray magnetic fields? If so, press it.
64	D	When the display settings don't work, you can easily return to standard VGA settings called VGA mode, which includes a resolution of 640 × 480.
65	B	Although not an essential tool, a POST diagnostic card, also called a POST card, or motherboard test card, can be of great help to discover and report computer errors and conflicts that occur when you first turn on a computer and before the operating system (such as Windows 7) is launched.
66	D	Although not an essential tool, a POST diagnostic card, also called a POST card, or motherboard test card, can be of great help to discover and report computer errors and conflicts that occur when you first turn on a computer and before the operating system (such as Windows 7) is launched.
67	C	To understand what a POST card does, you need to know about the programs and data stored on the motherboard called the BIOS (basic input/output system).
68	B	The BIOS programs are stored on a special ROM (read-only memory) chip.
69	A	The BIOS programs are stored on a special ROM (read-only memory) chip. Because these embedded programs are so closely tied to the hardware, they are called firmware.
70	D	System BIOS manages essential devices (such as the keyboard, mouse, hard drive, and monitor) before the OS is launched.
71	A	Startup BIOS is used to start the computer.
72	C	BIOS setup or CMOS setup is used to change the motherboard configuration or settings.
73	D	The POST (power-on self test) is a series of tests performed by the startup BIOS when you first turn on a computer.
74	B	A power supply tester is used to measure the output of each connector coming from the power supply.
75	C	A multimeter is a general-purpose tool that can measure several characteristics of electricity in a variety of devices.
76	A	Continuity determines that two ends of a cable or fuse are connected without interruption.
77	B	A loopback plug is used to test a port in a computer or other device to make sure the port is working and might also test the throughput or speed of the port.

B

Question	Answer	Explanation
78	D	A loopback plug is used to test a port in a computer or other device to make sure the port is working and might also test the throughput or speed of the port.
79	C	The term booting comes from the phrase "lifting yourself up by your bootstraps" and refers to the computer bringing itself up to a working state without the user having to do anything but press the on button.
80	A	A hard boot, or cold boot, involves turning on the power with the on/off switch.
81	D	A hard boot, or cold boot, involves turning on the power with the on/off switch.
82	B	A soft boot, or warm boot, involves using the operating system to reboot.
83	A	A hard boot initializes the processor and clears memory.
84	C	A successful boot depends on the hardware, the BIOS, and the operating system all performing without errors.
85	B	EFI (Extensible Firmware Interface) and UEFI (Unified EFI) are two standards for the interface between firmware on the motherboard and the operating system. The standards replace the legacy BIOS standards and improve on processes for booting, handing over the boot to the OS, and loading device drivers and applications before the OS loads.
86	A	The MBR program contains the partition table and the master boot program used to locate and start the BootMgr program.
87	D	The Boot Configuration Data file is organized the same as a registry hive and contains boot settings that control BootMgr, WinLoad.exe, WinResume.exe (when resuming from hibernation), MemTest.exe (when memory is tested), and dual boots.
88	A	The MBR program searches the partition table for the active partition, which Windows calls the system partition.
89	C	When starting XP, the MBR looks for the first sector in the active partition, which is called the OS boot record.
90	A	Ntldr reads XP settings used for the boot stored in Boot.ini.
91	C	Safe Mode boots the OS with a minimum configuration and can be used to solve problems with a new hardware installation, a corrupted Windows installation, or problems caused by user settings.
92	D	Use System Configuration to disable unneeded services or startup processes.
93	B	Use the chkdsk /r command to check for file system errors.

Question	Answer	Explanation
94	C	Windows Recovery Environment (Windows RE) is a lean operating system that can be launched to solve Windows startup problems after other tools available on the Advanced Boot Options menu have failed to solve the problem.
95	A	Try to repair a corrupted file system by using the command prompt window and the chkdsk c: /r command.
96	C	Use a SATA-to-USB converter to recover data from a drive using a SATA connector.
97	A	A cable tester can be used to test a cable to find out if it is good or to find out what type of cable it is if the cable is not labeled.
98	A	You can use a cable tester to trace a network cable through a building.
99	C	A loopback plug can be used to test a network cable or port. Whereas a cable tester works on cables that are not live, a loopback plug works with live cables.
100	B	A wireless locator helps you find a Wi-Fi hotspot and tells you the strength of the RF signal.
101	C	The ping (Packet InterNet Groper) command tests connectivity by sending an echo request to a remote computer.
102	D	The ipconfig (IP configuration) command can display TCP/IP configuration information and refresh the TCP/IP assignments to a connection including its IP address.
103	A	Ipconfig /renew leases a new IP address from a DHCP server.
104	C	Ipconfig /all displays TCP/IP information.
105	B	Nslookup (name space lookup) lets you read information from the Internet name space by requesting information about domain name resolutions from the DNS server's zone data.
106	D	Control Message Protocol (ICMP) messages are used by routers and hosts to communicate error messages and updates.
107	C	To check for local connectivity, use Windows Explorer to try to access shared folders on the network.
108	A	To find out if a computer with limited or no connectivity was able to initially connect to a DHCP server on the network, check for an Automatic Private IP Address (APIPA).
109	D	A computer assigns itself an APIPA if it is unable to find a DHCP server when it first connects to the network. Use the ipconfig command to find out the IP address.

B

Question	Answer	Explanation
110	B	If the router or switch is in a server closet and the ports are not well labeled, you can use a loopback plug to find out which port the computer is using.
111	A	Intermittent connectivity on a wired network might happen when a network device such as a VoIP phone is sensitive to electrical interference. You can solve this problem by attaching a ferrite clamp on the network cable near the phone port. This clamp helps to eliminate electromagnetic interference (EMI).
112	C	If you are having a problem accessing a particular computer on the Internet, try using the tracert command. The results show computers along the route that might be giving delays.
113	D	To see the priority order and find out which connection is faster, use the Networking tab of Task Manager.
114	A	If you encounter a problem when installing Windows 7 using RAID or SCSI drives, such as a RAID or SCSI hard drive is not detected, know that the problem is a hardware or firmware problem and not a Windows setup problem.
115	C	If the system is experiencing a marked decrease in performance, suspect a virus and use up-to-date antivirus software to perform a full scan of the system.
116	B	In a Windows system, make sure at least 15 percent of drive C: is free.
117	C	If the performance problem still exists in Safe Mode, you can assume that the problem is with hardware.
118	A	Now that you have the startup process clean, you will want to keep it that way. You can use several third-party tools to monitor any changes to startup. A good one is WinPatrol by BillP Studios (www.winpatrol.com).
119	D	Many antivirus programs monitor the startup process and inform you when changes are made.
120	C	Use the System Information Utility (msinfo32.exe) to find information about the installed processor and its speed, how much RAM is installed, and free space on the hard drive.
121	B	The Windows 7/Vista indexer is responsible for maintaining an index of files and folders on a hard drive to speed up Windows searches.
122	A	If you notice that performance slows after a system has been up and running without a restart for some time, suspect a memory leak.
123	B	A memory leak is caused when an application does not properly release memory allocated to it that it no longer needs and continually requests more memory than it needs.

Question	Answer	Explanation
124	A	You can manually have Windows test a memory card or flash drive for ReadyBoost by right-clicking the device and selecting Properties from the shortcut menu.
125	C	The Windows Aero interface might be slowing down the system because it uses memory and computing power.
126	D	The Vista sidebar appears on the Windows desktop to hold apps called gadgets.
127	B	Most programs written for Windows have an uninstall routine that can be accessed from the Windows 7/Vista Programs and Features window, the XP Add Remove Programs window, or an uninstall utility in the All Programs menu.
128	A	Editing the registry can be dangerous, so do this with caution and be sure to back up first! Open the Registry Editor by using the regedit command in the search box.
129	C	To remove the program from the All Programs menu, right-click it and select Delete from the shortcut menu.
130	D	Restart the PC and watch for any startup errors about a missing program file. The software might have stored startup entries in the registry, in startup folders, or as a service that is no longer present and causing an error. If you see an error, use msconfig to find out how the program is set to start.

B